The Day of the LORD

The Bible's Fascinating Story of the End of This World and the Beginning of the Next

Joel 2:11b
The day of the LORD is indeed great and very awesome,
And who can endure it?

REVISED SECOND EDITION WITH STUDY GUIDE

by

Edwin K. (Ed) Nolan

Copyright © 2016 by Edwin K. Nolan. All rights reserved.

Except for quotations clearly noted from other translations, all Scripture quotations taken from the New American Standard Bible®,
Copyright © 1960, 1962, 1963, 1968, 1971, 1972, 1973, 1975, 1977, 1995 by The Lockman Foundation
Used by permission. (www.Lockman.org)

TIMELINE OF FUTURE EVENTS

"THE DAY OF THE LORD" (Revelation 5:7-20:15)

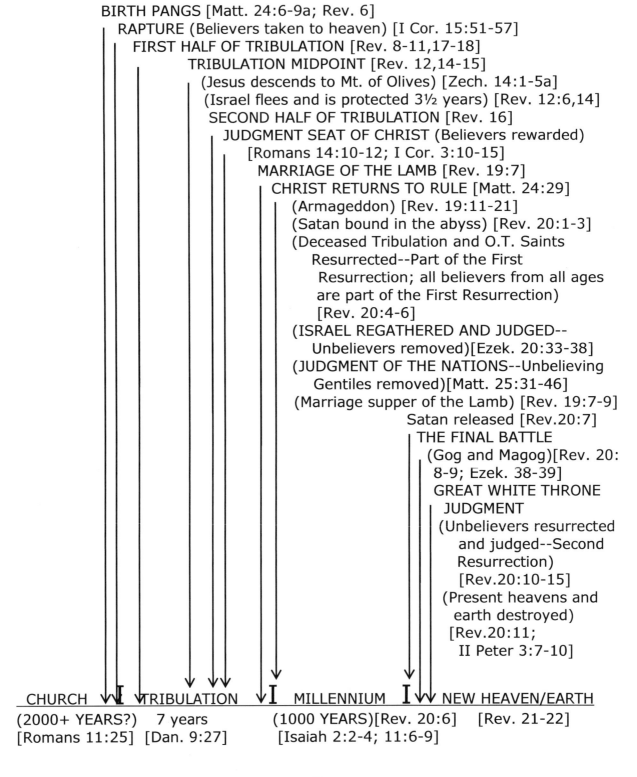

TABLE OF CONTENTS

Preface	4
Principles	5
Chapter 1: After Physical Death	10
Chapter 2: The Day of the LORD	16
Chapter 3: The Beginning of Birth Pangs	22
Chapter 4: The Rapture of the Church	25
Chapter 5: The Unholy Trinity	32
Chapter 6: The First Half of the Tribulation	40
Chapter 7: BABYLON THE GREAT	47
Chapter 8: The Tribulation Midpoint	52
Chapter 9: The Last Half of the Tribulation	60
Chapter 10: The Judgment Seat of Christ	64
Chapter 11: The Marriage of the Lamb	68
Chapter 12: Christ Returns to Rule	72
Chapter 13: The Millennial Kingdom	86
Chapter 14: The Final Battle	100
Chapter 15: The Great White Throne	109
Chapter 16: Eternity in the New Jerusalem	115
Acknowledgements	121

PREFACE

Dear Reader,

Thank you for considering this book. It is my prayer that it will assist you in looking to the Scriptures, and not to the commentaries, as your primary source for understanding end times prophecy.

Too many Christians aren't interested in end times prophecy because they think it is all found in the book of Revelation, which devotes most of its chapters to the "doom and gloom" of the terrible seven-year tribulation period. Why dwell on all that bad news? The truth is, however, that the prophecies contain a wealth of wonderful news about the future for believers, and should be a source of inspiration and joy to **"all who have loved His appearing." 2 Timothy 4:8.**

The message of the end times Biblical prophecies is one of hope, joy and assurance for every believer. God's love and provision for His children shine through virtually every prophetic passage, as we view the future we would have without His saving grace, and the joyful, glorious future with Him that He has prepared for us. It is not the end, but a glorious new beginning of eternity.

The many passages throughout the Bible describing the wonderful future our God has planned for us have certainly been an inspiration and a source of great joy, comfort and assurance to me. It is my pleasure and honor to share them with you.

Ed Nolan
January 2016

PRINCIPLES FOR THE STUDY OF BIBLE PROPHECY

MAIN IDEA: This book quotes many of the Bible's end times prophetic passages, with a narrative tying them to specific end times events in chronological order. It is written from the viewpoint that: (1) <u>Christians should continually attempt to understand prophecy directly from the Bible with the guidance of the Holy Spirit;</u> (2) end times prophecy is not limited to the book of Revelation, but is found throughout the Bible; (3) the Bible is the true, inerrant, inspired Word of God; and (4) the Bible, including all prophecy, is to be read literally unless a symbolic meaning is obvious.

1.

Acts 17:10-11: The brethren immediately sent Paul and Silas away by night to Berea, and when they arrived, they went into the synagogue of the Jews. Now these were more noble-minded than those in Thessalonica, for they received the word with great eagerness, <u>examining the Scriptures daily *to see* whether these things were so.</u> [New American Standard Bible (NASB) used with permission—All quotations are from NASB unless otherwise noted, and <u>all underlining is the author's, added for emphasis</u>.]

The Jews of Thessalonica thought they already knew the Scriptures. They did not need to examine them to determine if Paul and Silas were speaking God's truth; they rejected the message of Paul and Silas based on what they already knew. Or thought they knew. They rejected their preaching on the basis of their <u>preconceptions</u> of what the Word of God said and meant. And they missed the message of Psalm 22, Isaiah 49: 5-7; Isaiah 53, Micah 5:2 and the many, many other verses that Jesus explained to the two disciples on the road to Emmaus (Luke 24:27). But before explaining the prophecies to them, He admonished them in **Luke 24:25: "O foolish men and slow of heart to believe in all that the prophets have spoken."**

Many of His disciples have the same problem today. Many who have read commentaries on prophecy often believe that they understand God's revealed plan for the future and tend to reject without examination any suggestion that their understanding may not align with what the prophecies actually say, just as the Thessalonians apparently did according to Acts 17. The Thessalonian Jews were blinded by their <u>preconceptions</u> and would not reexamine the Scriptures, because they thought they could not possibly be wrong. <u>Do not be blinded by that conceit.</u> If a Scripture discussed in this book suggests a different understanding of an end times event than the one you currently have, do what the Bereans did: examine the Scriptures <u>to see whether it is so</u>.

On the other end of the spectrum, the vast majority of today's laymen are so discouraged by the difficulty of untangling the confusing web of prophecy found scattered throughout the Bible that they either avoid eschatology altogether, or rely solely on what they read in the commentaries or hear from their Bible teachers or pastors. For clarification, the word "eschatology" as used here, means the study of prophecy of events that have not yet happened, especially end times prophecy, also called apocalyptic literature (from the Greek word *apocalypse*, meaning an unveiling or revealing).

Some people excuse their avoidance of eschatology by joking, calling themselves "*pantheists,"* saying that "It will all pan out in the end." Others tend to consider themselves "experts" on prophecy, ignoring the fact that an "ex" is a has-been, and a "spurt" is a drip under pressure. Seriously, don't let your fear of not being able to understand prophetic passages keep you from reading the Scriptures themselves. As discussed below, you have the One who gave those passages to the prophets right there with you to help you understand them.

The author encourages the reader to put aside all preconceptions concerning unfulfilled prophecy and take a fresh, discerning look at Bible prophecy focused solely on what is found in the Bible itself. This is not a rehash of past commentaries on prophecy or a summary of "prevailing views" among Bible scholars. Commentaries and the current views among Bible scholars are not Scripture, and therefore, all commentaries (including this one) should not be considered to be without error. This book does not examine all the various views on Bible prophecy put forth by Bible scholars over the last 2000 years. The only works considered and examined in this book are those found in the Old and New Testaments.

I Cor. 2:12, 14: Now we [believers] **have received not the spirit of the world, but the Spirit who is from God, so that we may know the things freely given to us by God.... But the natural** [nonbeliever, unsaved] **man does not accept the things of the Spirit of God, for they are foolishness to him, and he cannot understand them....**

Can anyone truly understand any Scripture, let alone end times prophecy, apart from the guidance of the Holy Spirit? Jesus tells His disciples in **John 16:13: "But when He, the Spirit of truth, comes, He will guide you into all the truth; for He will not speak on His own initiative, but whatever He hears, He will speak; and He will disclose to you what is to come.**

The believer is encouraged to approach every verse of Scripture in the same manner one takes communion. Search out and confess all unconfessed sin (1 John 1:9), and seek the control and guidance of the Holy Spirit before opening God's Word. The goal of this book is to encourage laymen to trust the Scriptures and the guidance of the Holy Spirit, not the commentaries, as the primary source of the truth about the end times.

The chronological order of future events herein is based on the author's understanding of the relevant Scripture. That subject has created disagreement among Bible scholars, beginning prior to Christ's first coming and continuing today.

Today scholars cannot even agree on if, or when, an event as important as the event Bible scholars call the "rapture" of the church occurs. This book examines what the Scriptures say about the future occurrence and timing of each prophesied end times event for the reader's consideration.

Whether the reader ultimately sees the details of a prophesied end times event or its timing the same way the author does is not the objective. The primary concern is that <u>the reader reads the actual Scriptures</u> and acquires the spiritual maturity and knowledge needed to avoid falling prey to the many false teachers and false prophets in the world today:

Ephesians 4:11-15: And He gave some as apostles, and some as prophets, and some as evangelists, and some as pastors and teachers, for the equipping of the saints for the work of service, to the building up of the body of Christ; until we all attain to the unity of the faith, and of the knowledge of the Son of God, to a mature man, to the measure of the stature which belongs to the fullness of Christ. As a result, <u>we are no longer to be children, tossed here and there by waves and carried about by every wind of doctrine</u>, by the trickery of men, by craftiness in deceitful scheming; but speaking the truth in love, we are to grow up in all *aspects* **into Him who is the head,** *even* **Christ....**

2.

Too many Christians assume that end times prophecy is found <u>only</u> in the book of Revelation, when in fact end times prophecy is a central theme of many Old Testament prophetic books and such prophecies are mentioned in many New Testament books. To present just an overview of end times prophecy, this book contains quotations from many books of the Bible, including:

<u>Old Testament</u>
- Genesis
- Deuteronomy
- Job
- Isaiah
- Jeremiah
- Ezekiel
- Daniel
- Hosea
- Joel
- Zephaniah
- Zechariah
- Malachi

<u>New Testament</u>
- Matthew
- Mark
- Luke

John
Acts
Romans
1 Corinthians
Ephesians
Philippians
1 & 2 Thessalonians
1 & 2 Timothy
Hebrews
2 Peter
Revelation

Examining the end times prophecies of the Bible <u>as a whole</u> guards against an incomplete or inaccurate understanding of what the Scriptures actually tell us about the future.

3.

2 Timothy 3:16-17: All Scripture is inspired by God and profitable for teaching, for reproof, for correction, for training in righteousness; so that the man of God may be adequate, equipped for every good work.

It is beyond the scope of this work to discuss all the reasons we believe that all Scripture is contained in the Old and New Testaments of the Bible we have today, why we believe they are inerrant as originally written, and why we believe that the essence of those original writings is preserved in the manuscripts and translations we have today. These beliefs are the foundation for this book.

4.

II Peter 1:20-21: But know this first of all, that no prophecy in Scripture is *a matter* [italics indicate words in the NASB not found in the original manuscripts, but added for clarification in the English translation] **of one's own interpretation, for no prophecy was ever made by an act of human will, but men moved by the Holy Spirit spoke from God.**

Peter is saying that all prophecy will be fulfilled exactly according to God's plan, regardless of how the prophecy is interpreted by men. This passage makes it clear that if men have interpreted prophecy to have conflicting meanings, no more than one interpretation can be a correct understanding of God's revealed plan.

All fulfilled prophecy in Scripture has been fulfilled literally, not symbolically. Therefore, this book adheres to the literal, "historical/grammatical" approach to scripture, *i.e.,* the plain language of the passage at the time it was written is what it is meant, unless it is clearly symbolic or the meaning is explained later. For example, Christ's parables are clearly stories told to show some underlying truth, sometimes difficult to ascertain, and some are actually explained later to his disciples, as the parable of the sower is explained in Matthew 13:18-23. Some of the prophetic visions in the writings of the prophets are given in symbolic form and explained later. For examples, see Daniel 7:15-27 and Revelation 17:8-18.

This book is not an exhaustive study of end times prophecy and does not attempt to discuss all Scripture passages on the subject, or to deal with all the questions and speculations raised by the many existing commentaries. It is intended to be a short handbook introducing the layman to enough relevant Scripture to enable him to begin his own study of the Scriptures on end times prophecy: to rely on the Word of God, not the words of men. Put aside your preconceptions and allow the Holy Spirit to reveal to you the meaning of what He has inspired men to write about the future.

FOR REVIEW:

1. What is the primary thing the author wants the reader to learn from this book?

_____

2. The author assumes that: (check all that are true)
    a. all prophecy is symbolic.
    b. the books of the Bible are all writings inspired by God.
    c. only Bible scholars can understand prophecy directly from the Bible
    d. Bible prophecy should be read literally, unless a symbolic meaning is clearly indicated.
    e. prophetic passages can be read and understood by the layman.
    f. Christians can understand the true meaning of Scripture without the guidance of the Holy Spirit.

3. If two people have a different interpretation of the timing of a prophesied end times event, can they both be right?

_____

4. Most of the end times prophecies are found in the book of Revelation. True False

5. Did you learn anything you found significant in this chapter? Describe.

_____

CHAPTER ONE
AFTER PHYSICAL DEATH

MAIN IDEA: The Bible tells us that we have life beyond our physical death, with those who have received God's gift of salvation experiencing an eternity of joy in the presence of God and all others spending eternity in torment.

[I]t is appointed for men to die once and after this *comes* judgment. Hebrews 9:27.

The first future event described in the Bible that most of us will probably experience is life after physical death. Most people avoid the unpleasant prospect of their own death. Many believers think that they are not going to die, but will be "raptured" as described in I Corinthians 15:51 *et seq*, not theologically a bad position in light of **Hebrews 9:28: Christ...will appear a second time for salvation without *reference to* sin** [*i.e.,* not to judge sin]**, to those who eagerly await Him.** (The event we call the "rapture" will be discussed in a later chapter.) However, death, like taxes, must be experienced by all of us, unless we are one of those believers alive at the time of the "rapture."

When people do think about death, and what the Bible says happens after death, they have many questions, such as:
1. Is physical death the end of consciousness, or is there conscious life after death?
2. If there is conscious life after death, what is it like?
3. Does the Bible really say there is a heaven and a hell?
4. Does the Bible definitely say what people have to do to go to heaven and what causes people to go to hell?
5. Is there such a thing as purgatory or "soul sleep"?
6. What is it like in heaven and hell?

This chapter will examine the answers we find in the Bible about what happens immediately after death. Later chapters will tell of an even more glorious future for the believer, and an even sadder one for the unbeliever.

I
Physical Death

So what is physical death? From the Biblical standpoint, it is the separation of the soul from the body (James 2:26). Let us examine physical death from the question of what has happened to those who have already died. Where are they now, according to the Scriptures?

In Luke 16:19-31, Jesus tells us about a beggar named Lazarus and a rich man, who both died, and the rich man went to Hades (the Greek word for the underworld, where the souls of the dead resided): **"In Hades he lifted up his eyes, being in torment, and saw Abraham far away and Lazarus in his bosom. And he cried out and said, 'Father Abraham, have mercy on me, and send Lazarus so that he may dip the tip of his finger in water and cool off my tongue, for I am in agony in this flame.'" Luke 16:23-24.** If anyone would know what happens when a person dies, it would be Jesus, who is God and the Creator of the universe (John 1:1-3, 14). Whether this is a parable or not, Jesus would not be "just kidding" about something this important.

The rich man obviously represents the unbeliever. John the Baptist tells his disciples in **John 3:36** [NKJV]: **"Whoever believes in the Son has everlasting life; and he who does not believe the Son shall not see life, but the wrath of God abides on him."**

Unfortunately for the rich man in Luke 16:23-24, and all unbelievers from the beginning of the human race until its end, here we see what the wrath of God looks like for all unbelievers after death. As much as the portrayal of unbelievers spending eternity in fiery torment may seem "insensitive and offensive," it is, sad to say for unbelievers, Biblically correct.

No amount of wishful thinking can change that fact. The Bible tells us there are NOT many paths to heaven. God does NOT grade on the curve ("If I'm good enough..."). There are only two kinds of people in God's eyes, as pictured by the two thieves on the crosses, one on each side of Jesus (John 19:18): the believer and the unbeliever. In **John 3:16-18,** Jesus explains it to Nicodemus this way: **"For God so loved the world, that He gave His only begotten Son, that whoever believes in Him shall not perish, but have eternal life. For God did not send the Son into the world to judge** [from the Greek word *krisis*, indicating condemnation] **the world, but that the world might be saved through Him. He who believes in Him is not judged** [condemned]**; he who does not believe has been judged** [condemned] **already, because he has not believed in the name of the only begotten Son of God...."** See also John 1:11-13.

II
Spiritual Death

Spiritual death is the separation of the soul from God. <u>We are all born as unbelievers, spiritually dead</u>: Let that sink in. You and I were born <u>separated from God</u>. **And you were dead in your trespasses and sins. Ephesians 2:1.** If Jesus, the Creator of the universe (Col.1:16) had not been born as a man and suffered and died to pay the penalty of death, both physical and spiritual, which is the penalty for sin (Romans 6:23), <u>all mankind would have been forever separated from God.</u> (See 2 Cor. 5:18.)

Because of His death on the cross, believers become spiritually alive by faith, by receiving God's gift of salvation through the work of Christ, who died for the sins of the world: **But God, being rich in mercy, because of His great love with which He loved us, even when we were** [spiritually] **dead in our transgressions, made us** [spiritually] **alive together with Christ (by grace you have been saved).... Ephesians 2:5.** As Jesus told Nicodemus in **John 3:3, "Truly, truly, I say to you, unless one is born again** [*i.e.,* born spiritually after being born physically] **he cannot see the kingdom of God."**

III
Two Different Eternities

Throughout Biblical prophecy we see two entirely different futures after physical death: one for the believer, and one for the unbeliever, beginning with the future of those who have already died. We have seen the future of the unbeliever as exemplified by the rich man. The final destination of the unbeliever is described in the picture of the Great White Throne Judgment, the subject of a later chapter.

What about the believers who have died? We know that the believer is spiritually alive, that is, united, not separated, from God. The sentence begun in **Ephesians 2:5** (quoted above) continues: **and raised us up with Him** [Christ], **and seated us with Him in the heavenly *places* in Christ Jesus, so that in the ages to come He might show the surpassing riches of His grace in kindness toward us in Christ Jesus. Ephesians 2:6-7.**

Jesus has prepared a place for believers in heaven: **"In My Father's house are many dwelling places; if it were not so, I would have told you; for I go to prepare a place for you. If I go and prepare a place for you, I will come again and receive you to Myself, that where I am, *there* you may be also." John 14:2-3.**

That place is the heavenly city, the new Jerusalem: **But as it is they** [believers] **desire a better *country,* that is, a heavenly one. Therefore God is not ashamed to be called their God; for He has prepared a city for them. Hebrews 11:16. But you** [believers] **have come to Mount Zion and to the city of the living God, the heavenly Jerusalem.... Hebrews 12:22.** Note that the new Jerusalem is already in existence in heaven, a place prepared for believers to dwell in the presence of God after physical death. The new Jerusalem is described in Revelation 21 and 22, the subject of our last chapter.

So believers end up in heaven in the new Jerusalem with Christ. But do they have to wait until some future event, like the "rapture," Christ's return to rule, or the end of time to get there? Is there such a thing as "soul sleep" or purgatory?

Not according to Paul's epistles: **For to me, to live is Christ and to die is gain. But if *I am* to live *on* in the flesh, this *will mean* fruitful labor for me; and I do not know which to choose. But I am hard-pressed from both *directions*, having the desire to depart and be with Christ, for *that* is very much better.... Philippians 1:21-23.**

The Bible leaves no questions about what happens to a person's soul when he/she dies. The unbeliever's soul goes to a place of fiery torment and the believer's soul goes to the heavenly Jerusalem to be with Christ. As we shall see in later chapters, the souls of both believers and unbelievers will be united with their bodies in the future, the former to spend eternity in the new Jerusalem and the latter to spend eternity in eternal torment. Also the subject of a later chapter, we see that <u>God gives each person enough faith to choose his/her own eternal future</u>, so those who remain unbelievers are without excuse.

IV
From Death to Life

So how does someone become a believer? What exactly does it mean to "believe in the Son (Jesus)"? What must you believe about Jesus to become what the Bible calls a "believer"? What does it mean to "repent"?

A. Repent

The word "repent" literally means to "rethink" as in changing one's mind. In Biblical terms, in this context it means changing one's mind about who Jesus really is. He claimed to be the Son of God, the Savior (Messiah) who the Old Testament prophets said would come to die for the sins of all mankind. (Isaiah chapter 53, Isaiah 49:6, Job 19:25-27) To become a 'believer", a person would first have to believe that the Jesus of Nazareth who is the subject of the Gospels of Matthew, Mark, Luke and John is in fact who He claims to be: The prophesied Messiah, God incarnate (in the flesh, born as a man), who died on the cross for the sins of mankind and rose alive on the third day.

B. Receive

Speaking of Jesus, the apostle John tells us in **John 1:10-13: He was in the world, and the world was made through Him, and the world did not know Him. He came to His own, and those who were His own did not receive Him. <u>But as many as received Him, to them He gave the right to become children of God,</u>** *even* **to those who believe in His name, who were born, not of blood nor the will of the flesh nor the will of man, but of God.** This **born of God** is the spiritual birth Jesus was telling Nicodemus about in **John 3:3** when He said, **"Truly, truly, I say to you, unless one is born again he cannot see the kingdom of God."**

So what does it mean to "receive Him"? Another look at **John 3:16** (quoted above) tells us that God <u>gave</u> His only begotten Son so that **"whoever believes in Him shall not perish, but have eternal life."** Eternal life in the new Jerusalem with God is a <u>GIFT</u>. A gift cannot be earned. But it must be accepted, that is, received, to be effective. If someone gives you a new car, it doesn't benefit you in the least if you never pick up the keys he places on the table in front of you. The gift of your salvation, that Jesus bought at so great a price by His death on the cross, must be <u>received by you personally</u>, as the passage from John 1:10-13 quoted above plainly states.

C. Trust

Accepting that gift will require <u>faith</u>. Instead of relying on your own good deeds, or some religious system you have been taught since childhood, the Bible says <u>you must put all your trust for your eternal destiny</u> in the hands of the Living God by trusting His Son's work on the cross as payment for <u>all</u> your sins, past, present, and future. We read in Ephesians **2:8-9: For by grace** [unearned favor from God] **you have been save through faith; and that** [faith] **not of yourselves,** *it is* <u>**the gift of God**</u>**; not as a result of** [good] **works, so that no one may boast.** So <u>God gives us the faith we need</u> to accept His freely offered gift of salvation. We can't do any good deeds (works) to earn our salvation. On our own, we don't even have enough faith to receive God's gift of salvation.

Don't think you have enough faith to put<u> all your trust for your eternal destiny</u> in God's free gift of salvation paid for by Jesus' death on the cross? Remember, <u>the faith to receive that gift comes from God.</u> The appropriate action might be the prayer of the father of the demon-possessed son to Jesus **in Mark 9:24: "I do believe; help my unbelief."** Just ask for the faith. He will give it to you.

<u>FOR REVIEW</u>: (Cite a verse for all answers and all <u>True</u> answers)

1. According to the Bible, everyone goes to heaven when they die.   True   False

2. The Bible teaches that there are many paths to heaven.   True   False

3. The Bible tells us there is no life after physical death.   True   False

4. The Bible tells us that the souls of those who have received Christ as their personal savior will go to heaven immediately after they die.   True   False

5. A good person goes to heaven; a bad person goes to hell.   True   False

6. Salvation is a gift from God that cannot be earned by good works.   True   False

7. Believers will spend eternity with God in the new Jerusalem.   True   False

8. Unbelievers will spend eternity in torment.   True   False

9. Jesus said a person must be "born again" to see the kingdom of God. True False

10. The faith necessary to accept God's free gift of salvation comes from God.
    True   False

11. Were you encouraged or discouraged by the Bible verses discussed in this

chapter? Explain.

12. What did you learn about spiritual death from this chapter?

CHAPTER TWO
THE DAY OF THE LORD

MAIN IDEA: The **day of the Lord** comprises all prophesied end times events of Revelation 5:7-20:15 (See the Timeline Chart on page 2). It is a time when God the Father hands over authority to Jesus, God the Son. Main events include the rapture of the church, the tribulation, the second coming of Christ, the millennial kingdom, and the great white throne judgment.

Joel 2:1:
>Blow a trumpet in Zion,
>And sound an alarm on My holy mountain!
>Let all the inhabitants of the land tremble,
>For the <u>day of the Lord</u> is coming....

Joel 2:11b
>The <u>day of the Lord</u> is indeed great and very awesome,
>And who can endure it?

Isaiah 2:12a:
>For <u>the Lord</u> of hosts will have a <u>day</u> *of reckoning*
>Against everyone who is proud and lofty....

Isaiah 13:6-9:
>Wail, for the <u>day of the Lord</u> is near!
>It will come as destruction from the Almighty.
>Therefore all hands will fall limp.
>And every man's heart will melt.
>They will be terrified.
>Pains and anguish will take hold of *them*;
>They will writhe like a woman in labor,
>They will look at one another in astonishment,
>Their faces aflame.
>Behold, the <u>day of the Lord</u> is coming,
>Cruel, with fury and burning anger,
>To make the land a desolation;
>And He will exterminate its sinners from it.

Jeremiah 30:7-9: [The Lord speaking, v.1]
>" 'Alas! for <u>that day</u> is great,
>There is none like it;
>And it is a time of Jacob's distress,
>But he will be saved from it.
>It shall come about on <u>that day</u>,' declares the Lord of hosts, 'that I will

break his yoke from off their [Israel's] neck and will tear off their bonds; and strangers shall no longer make them their slaves. But they shall serve the LORD their God and David their king, whom I will raise up for them....' "

Joel 3:18:
> And it will come about in <u>that day</u>
> That the mountains will drip with sweet wine,
> And the hills will flow with milk,
> And all the brooks of Judah will flow with water;
> And a spring will go out from the house of the LORD
> To water the valley of Shittim.

Isaiah 24:21-23:
> So it will happen in <u>that day</u>,
> That the LORD will punish the host of heaven on high,
> And the kings of the earth on earth.
> They will be gathered together
> *Like* prisoners in the dungeon,
> And will be confined in prison;
> And after many days they will *be* punished.
> Then the moon will be abashed and the sun ashamed,
> For the Lord of host will reign on Mount Zion and in Jerusalem,
> And *His* glory will be before His elders.

2 Thessalonians 2:1-2: Now we request you, brethren, with regard to the coming of our Lord Jesus Christ and our gathering together to Him, that you not be quickly shaken from your composure or be disturbed either by a spirit or a message or a letter as if from us, to the effect that <u>the day of the Lord</u> has come.

These are just a few of the many references to **the day of the LORD** (sometimes referred to as **that day**) found in the writings of the prophets. While some of the references referred to events coming in the prophet's immediate future (now long past), most referred to an eschatological time that is yet to come.

So Who is **the LORD**? What exactly does **the day of the LORD** mean? And what time period does it encompass in the future events predicted in the Bible?

<u>1. Who is "the LORD"?</u>

a. The phrase **the LORD** in the NASB is usually a translation of the Hebrew word "YHWH" (which we pronounce "Yahweh"), a word closely connected with **I AM** of the burning bush in Exodus 3:14-15. The name YHWH, which is translated in English Bibles as **the LORD**, is revealed to Moses in Exodus 6:2. YHWH is also associated with the words Redeemer and Savior in the Old Testament, where YHWH is used over 6,000 times.

The story of the New Testament is about YHWH being born of a virgin, wholly man and wholly God. **John 1:14a: And the Word became flesh, and dwelt among us....** Jesus told the Pharisees in **John 8:58, "Truly, truly, I say to you, before Abraham was born, I am."**

The Pharisees knew He was claiming to be YHWH. In the next verse, we see that they **picked up stones to throw at Him**, in an apparent attempt to stone Him for blasphemy. When used in the eschatological sense in the phrase **the day of the Lord**, **the Lord** refers to Jesus, the second member of the Trinity, also called **the Son of Man**. (Daniel 7:13)

New Testament writers clearly understood that **the Lord** in the phrase **the day of the Lord** was Jesus, and referred to future events that included His return:

2 Thessalonians 2:1-2: Now we request you, brethren, with regard to the coming of our Lord Jesus Christ and our gathering together to Him, that you not be quickly shaken from your composure or be disturbed either by a spirit or a message or a letter as if from us, to the effect that the day of the Lord has come.

Luke 17:24: [Jesus speaking] **"For just like the lightning, when it flashes out of one part of the sky, shines to the other part of the sky, so will the Son of Man be in His day."**

I Corinthians 1:7-8: ... so that you are not lacking in any gift, awaiting eagerly the revelation of our Lord Jesus Christ, who will also confirm you to the end, blameless in the day of our Lord Jesus Christ.

2. What exactly is **the day of the Lord**?

If **the Lord** is Jesus, then **the day of the Lord** would seem to be His day, a time when He has great authority, reclaims possession of the earth from Satan, establishes His kingdom on the earth, and finally judges all unbelievers at what we call the great white throne judgment of Revelation 20:11-15 (detailed in a later chapter). The following verses speak of such a time:

Matthew 11:27a: [Jesus speaking] **"All things have been handed over to Me by My Father;..."**

Matthew 28:18: And Jesus came up and spoke to them, saying, "All authority has been given to Me in heaven and on earth."

I Corinthians 15:25-28, 24: For He [Jesus] **must reign until He has put all His enemies under His feet. The last enemy that will be abolished is death. For He has put all things in subjection under His feet.** [quoting Psalm 8:6] **But when He says "All things are put in subjection," it is evident that He** [the Father] **is excepted who put all things in subjection to Him** [Jesus]. **When all things are subjected to Him, the Son Himself also will be**

subjected to the One [the Father] **who subjected all things to Him, so that God may be all in all.**
[Verse 24:] **Then comes the end, when He hands over the kingdom to the God and Father, when He has abolished all rule and all authority and power.**

3. What future time period does **the day of the LORD** cover? Or, to put it another way, what future events are part of **the day of the LORD**?

A review of the verses quoted above reveals that **the day of the LORD** covers, at the very least, the future events beginning with the "rapture" (snatching up) of the church in I Thessalonians 4:13-17 and ending with the establishment of **a new heaven and a new earth** in **Revelation 21:1**, thus including the events called the tribulation, the judgment seat of Christ, the second coming, the millennial kingdom, the great white throne judgment and the battle of Gog and Magog. Almost all of the future events described in prophecy prior to the new heaven and new earth of Revelation 21:1 are part of **the day of the LORD**.

The actual handing over of authority, which begins **the day of the LORD**, appears in **Revelation 5:1, 6-7, 11-12:** [1] **I saw in the right hand of Him who sat on the throne a book** [scroll] **written inside and on the back, sealed up with seven seals.... [6-7] And I saw between the throne (with the four living creatures) and the elders a Lamb standing, as if slain, having seven horns and seven eyes, which are the seven Spirits of God, sent out into all the earth. And He** [the Lamb, *i.e.*, Jesus] **came and took the book out of the right hand of Him who sat on the throne.** [11-12] **Then I looked, and I heard the voice of many angels around the throne and the living creatures and the elders; and the number of them was myriads of myriads, and thousands of thousands, saying with a loud voice, "Worthy is the Lamb that was slain to receive power and riches and wisdom and might and honor and glory and blessing."**

The scroll, having seven seals, is in the form of a Jewish last will and testament, which also had seven seals and could legally be opened (by breaking the seals) only by the heir. **Hebrews 1:1-2: God** [the Father] **... in these last days has spoken to us in His Son, whom He appointed heir of all things....** Thus we have Jesus presented as the legal heir to God the Father's apparent ultimate authority, with the right to break the seals on the scroll. If God the Father is handing over authority to the Son, then **the day of the LORD** begins at this point, and also includes the events of Revelation 6, described as **the beginning of birth pangs** (**Matthew 24:8**) in Chapter 3.

While almost all unfulfilled prophecy is mentioned (and sometimes described in great detail, *e.g.*, the millennial kingdom) by the Old Testament prophets, the timing of future events in relation to one another is often clarified by the words of Jesus and the book of Revelation in the New Testament. The entire Scriptures must be studied carefully to determine what will happen and the order in which each event will happen.

Jesus returns His ultimate authority to the Father after the great white throne judgment, when death, His last enemy (1 Corinthians 15:25) is thrown into the lake of fire in Revelation 20:14. This seems to be confirmed in **Revelation 22:3: There will no longer be any curse; and <u>the throne of God and of the Lamb will be in it</u>, and His bond-servants will serve Him; ...**

The timeline chart at the front of this book gives the author's understanding of the chronological order of future events, most of which take place in **the day of the LORD.** It is designed as a reference tool to orient the reader on the sequence of each significant event prophesied as it is discussed. It should be noted that the timing of some events is not clear, and opinions differ on the timing of some events in relation to other events, *e.g.*, whether the "rapture of the church" occurs before, during or after the tribulation period, the timing of the battle of Gog and Magog, etc. The timeline will therefore conflict with those used by others. However, this timeline is based solely on Scripture, without reference to or reliance on commentaries or tradition. Readers are encouraged to examine the Scriptures underlying each event and determine whether the timeline aligns with their understanding of the Scriptures.

<u>FOR REVIEW</u>: (Cite verses for your answers)

1. Old Testament prophets wrote about the day of the LORD. True False

2. Old Testament prophets all saw the day of the LORD as a terrible time.
   True False

3. Jesus is the LORD of the Old Testament born as a man, wholly man and wholly God. True False

4. What is the English translation of the Hebrew word written as YHWH? _____

5. Who is the heir of God the Father? _____

6. In what chapter of Revelation does the Father hand over authority to the Son?
   _____

7. In what chapter of Revelation does the Son return authority to the Father?
   _____

8. Jesus never claimed to be God, the great "I AM". True   False

9. The Apostle Paul prophesied about Jesus' time of authority. True False

10. The Apostle Paul never used the exact phrase "the day of the Lord." True False

11. According to the Bible, what is "The day of the Lord"?

_____

12. When do the Bible prophecies say the day of the Lord begins and ends?

_____

13. What does the Bible say about Jesus being present at the beginning of creation?

_____

_____

CHAPTER THREE
THE BEGINNING OF BIRTH PANGS

MAIN IDEA: In **Matthew 24:4-9a**, Jesus describes events that will precede the seven year tribulation period, calling them **"the beginning of birth pangs."** Revelation 6 appears to be an elaboration of these **"beginning of birth pangs**."

If we look at the timeline chart at the front of the book, we see the first end time event to occur during **the day of the LORD** is "birth pangs." In Matthew 24:3, the disciples ask Jesus to describe the sign of His coming and the end of the age. The terminology **the beginning of birth pangs** comes from His answer given in **Matt. 24:4-9a**: "And Jesus answered and said to them, "See to it that no one misleads you. For many will come in My name, saying, 'I am the Christ,' and will mislead many. You will be hearing of <u>wars and rumors of wars</u>. See that you are not frightened, for *those things* must take place, but *that* is not yet the end. For nation will rise against nation, and kingdom against kingdom and in various places there will be<u> famines</u> and <u>earthquakes</u>. But all these things are *merely* <u>the beginning of birth pangs</u>. Then** [after these things] **they will deliver you to tribulation...."

The events called **"the beginning of birth pangs"** by Jesus in this passage appear to be the same events described in detail in Chapter 6 of the book of Revelation. That chapter describes the future events that happen when the Lamb (Jesus) breaks the seven seals on the scroll He takes from the right hand of God the Father in Revelation 5:1-7.

<u>**"Wars and rumors of wars"**</u> happen in **Revelation 6:1-4: Then I** [John] **saw when the Lamb broke one of the seven seals, and I heard one of the four living creatures saying as with a voice of thunder, "Come." I looked, and behold, a white horse, and he who sat on it had a bow; and a crown was given to him, and he went out <u>conquering and to conquer</u>. When He broke the second seal, I heard the second living creature saying, "Come." And another, a red horse went out; and to him who sat on it, it was granted to <u>take peace from the earth</u>, and that** *men* **would slay one another; and a great sword was given to him.**

<u>Famine</u> and death resulting from the famine and wars are described in **Revelation 6:5-8: When He broke the third seal, I heard the third living creature saying, "Come." I looked, and behold, a black horse; and he who sat on it had a pair of scales in his hand. And I heard** *something* **like a voice in the center of the four living creatures saying, "A quart of wheat for a denarius, and three quarts of barley for a denarius** [ten times the normal prices because of the famine]**; and do not damage the oil and the wine." When the Lamb broke the fourth seal, I heard the voice of the fourth living**

creature saying, "Come." I looked, and behold, an ashen horse; and he who sat on it had the name Death; and Hades was following with him. Authority was given to them over a fourth of the earth, <u>to kill with sword and famine</u> and with pestilence and by the wild beasts of the earth.

A great <u>earthquake</u> is described in detail in **Revelation 6:12-14: I looked when He broke the sixth seal, and there was a great earthquake and the sun became black as sackcloth** *made* **of hair, and the whole moon became like blood; and the stars of the sky fell to the earth, as a fig tree casts its unripe figs when shaken by a great wind. The sky was split apart like a scroll when it is rolled up, and every mountain and island were moved out of their places.**

Revelation 6:2 may also be a reference to the antichrist being revealed, as Paul foretold in **2 Thess. 2:3: Let no one in any way deceive you, for** *it* [the **day of the Lord** (v.2), *i.e.*, the taking out of the church (believers), commonly referred to as "the rapture"] ***will not come*** **unless the apostasy comes first and the man of lawlessness is revealed, the son of destruction** [the antichrist]. Jesus may also be referring to the antichrist in the passage from Matthew 24 quoted above when He talks about many coming claiming to be the Christ.

Jesus' brief description of the prelude to the seven-year tribulation period, which He calls **"the beginning of birth pangs"** in **Matthew 24:4-9a** quoted above, mentions the same events described in greater detail in Revelation 6. The events described in Revelation 6, thought by many Bible scholars to be events occurring in the first half of the tribulation, are more likely to be events occurring <u>before</u> the tribulation begins, making them **"the beginning of birth pangs"** of **Matthew 24:4-9a**.

Revelation 6 ends with an <u>announcement of the impending tribulation</u>: **Then the kings of the earth and the great men and the commanders and the rich and the strong and every slave and free man hid themselves in the caves and among the rocks of the mountains; and they said to the mountains and to the rocks, "Fall on us and hide us from the presence of Him who sits on the throne, and from the wrath of the Lamb; <u>for the great day of their wrath has come</u>, and who is able to stand?" Rev. 6:15-17** This announcement is further evidence that the events John sees when the seven seals are broken are the prelude to the tribulation, and not part of the tribulation itself.

Note the similarity to **Isaiah 2:19:**

Men **will go into caves of the rocks**
And into holes of the ground
Before the terror of the Lord
And the splendor of His majesty,
When He arises to make the earth tremble.

One more note: In preparation for the tribulation, the 144,000 Jews are sealed with the seal of the living God on their foreheads <u>immediately</u> after the announcement of the impending tribulation in Rev. 6:16-17 cited above. The angel having the seal of God cries out to **"the four angels to whom it was granted to harm the earth and the sea, saying, "Do not harm the earth or the sea or the trees until we have sealed the bondservants of our God on their foreheads." Rev. 7:2-3.** This passage also seems to indicate that <u>the tribulation itself begins AFTER the sealing of the 144,000</u>, with the sounding of the trumpets in Rev. 8.

Will the true church live through these events on earth, or will the "rapture" have already occurred? While the answer is not clear, Jesus' words in Matt. 24:4-9 and Paul's prophecy in 2 Thess.2:3 seem to indicate that the church will experience these pre-tribulation events (**"the beginning of birth pangs"**) on earth. The description and timing of the "rapture" of the church is the subject of our next chapter.

<u>FOR REVIEW</u>: (Cite verses for your answers.)

1. Where do we find the phrase "the beginning of birth pangs"? _____

2. What three things happen on earth during "the beginning of birth pangs"?

_____

3. What verse in Revelation seems to announce the beginning of the tribulation? ___

4. Are the 144,000 sealed before, after, or during the tribulation? _____

5. What chapter in Revelation tells of events similar to those described as "the beginning of birth pangs" by Jesus in Matthew 24? _____

6. Will the church live through "the beginning of birth pangs" or will it have already been raptured?

_____

7. Discuss the possibility that "the beginning of birth pangs" has already begun.

_____

8. List your understanding of the sequence of events described in this chapter?

_____

CHAPTER FOUR
THE RAPTURE OF THE CHURCH

MAIN IDEA: Jesus' church, *i.e.,* all believers who lived from the day of Pentecost in Acts 2 until the "rapture" occurs, both those deceased and alive at the time of the event, will be transformed into immortal bodies and caught up to be with the Lord in the air.

A. What is the church?

Matthew 16:15-18: He [Jesus] **said to them** [the disciples], **"but who do you say that I am?**

Simon Peter answered, "You are the Christ, the Son of the living God."

And Jesus said to him, "Blessed are you, Simon Barjona, because flesh and blood did not reveal *this* **to you, but My Father who is in heaven. I also say to you that you are Peter, and upon this rock** [*i.e.,* the truth just spoken by Peter, that Jesus is the Christ] **I will build my church...."**

The word **"church"** literally means "a called out group or assembly", and that is Jesus' meaning here. The church is literally the group (or assembly) called by God to trust Him and Jesus' work on the cross for their eternal salvation, and to serve Him as bondservants (*e.g.,* 2 Timothy 2:24; Revelation 22:3). This "church" began with all believers alive on the day of Pentecost of Acts chapter 2, and will end its time in mortal bodies on this present earth when all believers since that day, both living and dead, are taken up in the event we call the "rapture."

B. What is the rapture of the church?

The word "rapture" comes from the Latin words *raptus* and *rapere*, which mean "to carry away." As used to describe the future rapture of the church, it has exactly that meaning **in I Corinthians 15:51-57:**

Behold, I tell you a mystery; we will not all sleep, but we will all be changed, in a moment, in the twinkling of an eye, at the last trumpet; for the trumpet will sound, and the dead will be raised imperishable, and we will be changed. For this perishable must put on the imperishable, and this mortal must put on immortality.
But when this perishable will have put on the imperishable, and this mortal will have put on immortality, then will come about the saying that is written, "Death is swallowed up in victory. O Death, where is your victory? O Death, where is your sting?"
The sting of death is sin, and the power of sin is the law; but thanks

be to God, who gives us the victory through our Lord Jesus Christ.

Paul gives us more details **in I Thessalonians 4:13-17:**

But we do not want you to be uninformed, brethren, about those who are asleep, so that you will not grieve as do the rest who have no hope. For if we believe that Jesus died and rose again, even so God will bring with Him those who have fallen asleep in Jesus.
For this we say to you by the word of the Lord, that we who are alive and remain until the coming of the Lord, will not precede those who have fallen asleep. For the Lord Himself will descend from heaven with a shout, with the voice of the archangel and with the trumpet of God, <u>and the dead in Christ will rise first. Then we who are alive and remain will be caught up together with them in the clouds to meet the Lord in the air</u>, and so we shall always be with the Lord.

Note that the event we call the "rapture" includes both a <u>resurrection</u> (a uniting of the soul and the body, which comes to life) of the dead believers who are members of the church, and a <u>transformation</u> of mortal bodies of all members of the church, both those resurrected and those alive at the time, into immortal ones, and their immediate removal from earth and placement in heaven.

Jesus referred to this future event **in John 14:1-3:**

"Do not let your heart be troubled; believe in God, believe also in Me. In My Father's house are many dwelling places; if it were not so, I would have told you; for I go to prepare a place for you. If I go and prepare a place for you, I will come again and receive you to Myself, that where I am, there you may be also."

Although the word "rapture" does not appear in English translations of the Bible, we use it here, to refer to this future event.

<u>C. What will our changed bodies be like?</u>

We know our changed bodies will be immortal from the first two passages quoted above. So what will this immortal body look like? We are given a hint in **Philippians 3:20-21: For our citizenship is in heaven, from which also we eagerly wait for a Savior, the Lord Jesus Christ; <u>who will transform the body of our humble state into conformity with the body of His glory</u>, by the exertion of power that He has even to subject all things to Himself.** Bible scholars often refer to our immortal bodies as "glorified bodies" based on this passage.

Christ, resurrected in His glorified body, was recognizable when He wished to be recognized (John 20:20; Luke 24:16, 31; John 21:12), was able to appear and disappear where and when He wished, even in locked rooms (John 20:19, 26; Luke 24:15, John 21:1-7; Acts 1:3), could talk, cook fish and even eat (Luke 24:41-42).

He has a physical body with supernatural powers, of which we see only a glimpse. To what extent our glorified bodies will conform to His is not specified, and would therefore be a topic for fruitless speculation.

D. Who will receive these glorified bodies?

According to these passages, those who are "in Christ," both living and dead, from the day of Pentecost in Acts 2 until the rapture occurs, will have their bodies transformed into immortal, imperishable bodies (conforming to Christ's glorified body) in an instant, and be caught up ("raptured") to meet the Lord Jesus "in the air."

So what does it mean to be "in Christ?" The entire Bible, and especially the New Testament, speaks to that question. Jesus answers that question for Nicodemus the Pharisee in John 3:1-21. (*e.g.,* **"Truly, truly I say to you, unless one is born again he cannot see the kingdom of God." John 3:3** Anyone who does not <u>know</u> that he is "in Christ" should stop and read those verses carefully before proceeding, in order to understand what the Bible is actually saying about the future. John the Baptist gives a shorthand version of the final result of being "in Christ" in **John 3:36:**

He that believeth on the Son hath everlasting life: and he that believeth not the Son shall not see life; but the wrath of God abideth on him. (King James Version)

<u>Those to be "caught up" then, are those who trust in Christ and His work on the cross for their salvation, and not on their own merit or goodness</u>. **John 1:12-13** puts it this way: **But as many as received Him** [*i.e.,* personally received His free gift of salvation], **to them He gave the right to become children of God, even to those who believe in His name, who were born,** [spiritually] **not of blood nor the will of the flesh nor of the will of man, but of God.**

The rapture, then, is an event that happens only to those who are truly "born again Christians." As noted above, this group, both living and already dead, who have believed during the time from the day of Pentecost in Acts 2 until the rapture actually occurs, is referred to as **the church.** Paul uses the word to refer to this group in **Ephesians 5:25-27:**

Husbands, love your wives, just as Christ also loved the church and gave Himself up for her, so that He might sanctify her, having cleansed her by the washing of water with the word, that He might present to Himself the church in all her glory, having no spot or wrinkle or any such thing; but that she would be holy and blameless.

E. When will the rapture of the church occur?

Bible scholars have disagreed on the answer to this question apparently since the day of Pentecost. Most opinions range from "any second now" to after the end of the tribulation at Christ's Second Coming, with some even believing the event occurs after the end of Christ's one thousand year reign on earth. The first question concerning the timing of the rapture is whether it takes place before, during or after the tribulation period, the seven-year period in which "the wrath of God" is poured out on the earth. No definitive answer is given in Scripture, but there are clues:

1. After describing the rapture in I Thessalonians 4:13-17 (above), Paul writes in **1 Thessalonians 5:9: For God has not destined us for wrath, but for obtaining salvation through our Lord Jesus Christ.** By itself, this could refer either to the rapture of the church before the tribulation begins, or to the eternal wrath of God suffered by unbelievers in the lake of fire (discussed later), but there are other clues.

2. **1 Thessalonians 1:9-10: For they themselves report about us what kind of a reception we had with you, and how you turned to God from idols to serve a living and true God, <u>and to wait for His Son from heaven</u>, whom He raised from the dead,** *that is* **Jesus, <u>who rescues us from the wrath to come</u>.** That **wrath to come** is the same phrase used when the men on earth announce the beginning of the tribulation with these words**: "...for the great day of their** [God the Father's and the Lamb's] **<u>wrath has come</u>, and who is able to stand?" Revelation 6:17.**

3. In **Revelation 3:10**, Jesus, speaking to the true (faithful, believing) local church at Philadelphia, says**: "Because you have kept the word of My perseverance, <u>I also will keep you from the hour of testing</u>, that** *hour* **which is about to come upon the whole world, <u>to test those who dwell on the earth</u>."** He appears to be saying two things here:
    a. The true church, as defined above, will be kept from **the hour of testing** (the seven-year tribulation period); and
    b. The **"hour of testing"** is to test **"those who dwell on the earth"**, a phrase which refers to unbelievers. The church need not be there, since the testing is not directed at them.

These verses seem to indicate that the true church will <u>not</u> be on the earth during the tribulation period, meaning that the rapture occurs before the actual tribulation period starts.

When we look at Revelation 6:9, we see the souls of martyred saints not yet in their glorified bodies, indicating that the rapture has not yet occurred during this period which Jesus called **"the beginning of birth pangs"** in **Matthew 24:8** (described in the previous chapter):

Revelation 6:9: When the Lamb broke the fifth seal, I saw underneath the altar the <u>souls</u> of those who had been slain because of the word of God, and because of the testimony which they had maintained; and they cried out with a loud voice, saying, "How long, O Lord, holy and true, will You <u>refrain from judging and avenging</u> our blood on those who dwell on the earth?"

Not only are the saints <u>not</u> in glorified bodies, indicating that the rapture has not yet occurred, their question indicates that the **wrath** [**Rev. 6:19**] of God, the tribulation period, has not yet begun.

4. Next, we see the church in heaven in **Revelation 7:9-10**:

After these things I looked, and behold, <u>a great multitude which no one could count, from every nation and *all* tribes and peoples and tongues</u>, standing before the throne and before the Lamb, clothed in white robes, and palm branches *were* in their hand; and they cry out with a loud voice, saying, "Salvation to our God who sits on the throne, and to the Lamb."

The sudden appearance of this **great multitude**, coupled with the description of the unressurected "souls" in Revelation 6:9, indicates that the raptured church is now in heaven, and the event occurred after Revelation 6:9. This multitude appears to be embodied, having feet and legs to stand on and hands to hold palm branches. (That appearance of embodiment by itself, however, would not be reliable confirmation that this multitude is indeed in glorified bodies since we have a similar description of the (probably martyred) tribulation saints standing and holding **harps of God** in **Revelation 15:2**. We are told that the tribulation saints do not come to life until Revelation 20:4, at Christ's return to rule, so they cannot be in their glorified bodied in Revelation 15:2.)

The **great multitude** of **Revelation 7:9-10** is identified in **Revelation 7:13-14**:

Then one of the elders answered, saying to me, "These who are clothed in the white robes, who are they, and where have they come from?" I said to him, "My lord, you know." And he said to me, "These are the ones who come out of the great tribulation, and they have washed their robes and made them white in the blood of the Lamb."

Note that at this point these saints are already in heaven, <u>and the tribulation has not yet begun</u>. It begins with the trumpet judgments in Revelation chapter 8. Furthermore, those believers who die during the tribulation do not **come to life** in their glorified bodies until Christ's "second coming" <u>at the end of the tribulation</u> (See **Revelation 20:4**), <u>and</u> are described separately (<u>after</u> they have been killed) in Revelation 15:2.

When we examine all the passages in this section 4 together, including the passages in 1 Thessalonians and those in Revelation, the conclusion is that this **great multitude** in **Revelation 7:9** is the raptured church, taken up <u>before</u> the tribulation has begun, thereby taking the church **out of the great tribulation**. **Revelation 7:14.** This conclusion places the rapture <u>after</u> **the beginning of birth pangs** in Revelation 6, and <u>before</u> the beginning of the tribulation in Revelation 8.

5. **2 Thessalonians 2:1-3: Now we request you, brethren, with regard to the**

coming of our Lord Jesus Christ and our gathering together to Him, [the rapture] **that you not be quickly shaken from your composure or be disturbed either by a spirit or a message or a letter as if from us, to the effect that the day of the Lord has come** [and you missed it]. **Let no one in any way deceive you, for *it*** [the rapture] ***will not come* until the apostasy comes first, and <u>the man of lawlessness is revealed</u>, the son of destruction** [the antichrist]**.**

According to this passage, the antichrist is to be revealed <u>before</u> the rapture takes place. His appearance seems to take place in **Revelation 6:2: I** [John] **looked, and behold, a white horse, and he who sat on it had a bow; and a crown was given to him, and he went out conquering and to conquer**. The prophet Daniel tells us concerning his seventieth "week" (literally, seven, meaning seven years) that the antichrist will make a peace treaty at the start of the week, which is the seven year tribulation period, indicating that he **is revealed** before the tribulation starts: "**And he** [the antichrist] **will make a firm covenant with the many** [nations] **for one week, but in the middle of the week he will put a stop to sacrifice and grain offering;..."** Daniel 9:27a.

In order to make a peace treaty with many nations, the antichrist must have acquired considerable territory and power before the start of the tribulation period, so his appearance and identity would be clear at that point, as indicated in 2 Thessalonians 2:1-3 above, placing the rapture after his appearance in Revelation 6:2.

These passages, taken together, seem to indicate that this **great multitude** in **Revelation 7:9** (quoted above) is the raptured church, placing the rapture <u>after</u> **the beginning of birth pangs [Matthew 24:8]** in Revelation 6, <u>after</u> **the man of lawlessness is revealed**, **[2 Thess. 2:3]** <u>and before</u> the beginning of the tribulation in Revelation 8.

The important thing to remember is that when the rapture of the church actually occurs, <u>all</u> living believers, *i.e.*, the church ("born again Christians"), with the possible exception of the 144,000 Jews mentioned in Revelation 7 and 14 and the two witnesses of Revelation 11, are transformed into immortal, glorified bodies and removed from the earth and taken to heaven. With those possible exceptions, only unbelievers will be left alive on earth immediately after the rapture. Later we will examine an event when all living <u>unbelievers</u> are removed from the earth.

With the church removed from the earth, God's attention once more focuses on His chosen people, Israel, as we shall see as we examine the events of Daniel's seventieth seven, the seven-year tribulation period.

<u>FOR REVIEW</u>: (Cite verses for your answers.)

1. What happens at the event we call the rapture? _____

2. What people are "caught up" in the rapture? _____

3. Where is Jesus during the rapture? _____

4. What verses support the view that the rapture occurs <u>before</u> the tribulation starts?

_____

5. What is "the wrath to come" of 1 Thessalonians 1:9-10? _____

6. Where will those who are "caught up" be after the rapture? _____

7. Describe the bodies of those who are "caught up" after the rapture occurs.

_____

8. Do you think the books and movies about the rapture portray it accurately? Why or why not?
_____

9. When will the rapture occur? _____

10. Are you looking forward to the rapture with anticipation or dread? Why?

_____

11, When does the church age begin and when does it end? _____

_____

CHAPTER FIVE
THE UNHOLY TRINITY

MAIN IDEA: The tribulation period is dominated by Satan's imitation of the Holy Trinity in the form of Satan himself as the anti-God the Father, a man called **the beast** coming out of a new Roman Empire as the anti-Christ, or antichrist, and his lieutenant, called **the false prophet**, as the anti-Holy Spirit.

In Revelation 13, we see Satan, **the dragon**, form his "unholy trinity" in an attempt to counterfeit the Godhead. He sets himself up as the anti-God the Father, with a man called **the beast** as the anti-Christ (the antichrist) and another man called **the false prophet** as the anti-Holy Spirit, with the antichrist ruling the whole world at the end of his conquest, in imitation of Christ's coming one thousand year reign after the tribulation, called the "kingdom age" in the Old Testament. In this chapter we will take a look at the origin, authority and actions of Satan and these two men who will be Satan's physical representatives on earth during the tribulation period.

A. Satan

Satan's original rebellion against God stemmed from his desire to be like, or equal to, God. Isaiah describes it in **Isaiah 14: 12-14:**

"How you have fallen from heaven,
O star of the morning, son of the dawn!
You have been cut down to earth,
You have weakened the nations!
"But you said in your heart,
'I will ascend to heaven;
I will raise my throne above the stars of God,
And I will sit on the mount of assembly
In the recesses of the north.
'I will ascend above the heights of the clouds;
I will make myself like the Most High.'..."

We are given a more complete description of Satan's origin and fall **in Ezekiel 28: 12b-17:** 'Thus says the Lord GOD,

"You had the seal of perfection,
Full of wisdom and perfect in beauty.
You were in Eden, the garden of God;
Every precious stone was your covering:
The ruby, the topaz and the diamond;

> The beryl, the onyx and the jasper;
> The lapis lazuli, the turquoise and the emerald;
> And the gold, the workmanship of your settings and sockets,
> Was in you.
> On the day that you were created
> They were prepared.
> You were <u>the anointed cherub who covers</u>,
> And I placed you *there*.
> You were on the holy mountain of God;
> You walked in the midst of the stones of fire. [See Ezekiel 1:13.]
> You were blameless in your ways
> From the day you were created
> Until unrighteousness was found in you.
> By the abundance of your trade
> You were internally filled with violence,
> And you sinned;
> Therefore I have cast you as profane
> From the mountain of God.
> And I have destroyed [removed] you,
> O covering cherub,
> From the midst of the stones of fire.
> Your heart was lifted up because of your beauty;
> You corrupted your wisdom by reason of your splendor.
> I cast you to the ground [earth];
> I put you before kings,
> That they may see you...."'

This rebellion must have taken place before Satan's appearance in the Garden of Eden in Genesis 3. Beginning at that point, Satan has been the enemy of God and the deceiver of mankind, the embodiment of evil in all its seductive and horrific forms for the entire history of the human race. These passages make it clear that Satan is a cherub (an angelic being guarding the throne of God, see Ezekiel 1:5-28, 10:1-22), an individual, sentient being now leading his angelic forces (perhaps a third of the total angelic hosts, see Revelation 12:4a) in continuous and unrelenting rebellion against God.

Revelation 12:3: Then another sign appeared in heaven: and behold, a great red dragon having seven heads and ten horns, and on his head *were* seven diadems.

Revelation 12:9a: And the great dragon was thrown down, the serpent of old who is called the devil and Satan,....

Revelation 13:1a: And the dragon stood on the sand of the seashore.

So Satan sets himself up as the enemy of God before he tempts Eve in the Garden of Eden. But why does Satan form his "unholy trinity" and set up the antichrist as a dictator who insists on being worshiped as a god and who ends up ruling the entire earth during the last part of the tribulation period?

Satan can read prophecy. He knows that God's plan is for Jesus to reign on earth during the 1000 year period the Old Testament prophets and Jesus called **"the kingdom of God"** (See John 3:3). Satan's formation of his "unholy trinity" is an attempt to counterfeit that rule. Whether his ultimate goal is actually to challenge God, or just to vent his anger toward God by wreaking death and destruction on the earth (directed especially at tribulation believers) is unclear, but the latter seems likely in view of his defeat in heaven at the tribulation midpoint, to be discussed later.

B. The antichrist

Paul tells us that the tribulation will not come until after **the man of lawlessness is revealed. 2 Thessalonians 2:3.** The antichrist is thought to appear as the man on the white horse (a counterfeit of Jesus' appearance at the battle of Armageddon) in Revelation 6:2. The angel Gabriel tells Daniel in **Daniel 9:27** that **"he** [the antichrist] **will make a firm covenant with the many** [nations] **for one week,..."**

This passage from Daniel indicates that the antichrist has political power at the start of the tribulation period. Otherwise, he would not be in a position to make such a peace treaty.

However, the antichrist and the details of his Satanic rule during the seven-year tribulation period are not described until Revelation 13, between details given of the tribulation midpoint in heaven in Revelation 12 and on earth in Revelation 14. This may indicate that the antichrist and his false prophet are not indwelled by Satan and/or demons until the tribulation midpoint, in preparation for their reign of horror during the last half of the tribulation. Or, this delayed description of Satan's unholy trinity may be because it does not greatly impact Israel until shortly before the tribulation midpoint. The antichrist does not break his **firm covenant with the many** and conquer many countries, including Israel, until **the middle of the week** (Daniel 9:27). God's focus is on Israel during the tribulation period.

1. *The antichrist's power and authority*

Note in the passage below that the antichrist's **authority to act** is limited to forty-two months, suggesting that the worst horrors of his rule take place during the last one-half of the seven-year tribulation, what Jesus called **"a great tribulation"** in **Matthew 24:21**, when the antichrist rules almost the whole world. Certainly his impact on the nation of Israel (which is God's focus during this time) is not felt until the last half of the tribulation.

Revelation 13: 1b-8:
Then I saw a beast coming up out of the sea, having ten horns and seven heads, and on his horns *were* **ten diadems** [crowns of authority]**, and on his heads** *were* **blasphemous names. And the beast which I saw was**

like a leopard, and his feet were like *those* of a bear, and his mouth like the mouth of a lion. <u>And the dragon gave him his power and his throne and great authority.</u> *I saw* one of his heads as if it had been slain, and his fatal wound was healed. And the whole earth was amazed *and followed* after the beast; they worshiped the dragon because he gave his authority to the beast; and they worshiped the beast, saying, "Who is like the beast, and who is able to wage war with him?"

There was given to him a mouth speaking arrogant words and blasphemies, and <u>authority to act for forty-two months</u> [the last half of the tribulation period] <u>was given to him.</u> And he opened his mouth in blasphemies against God, to blaspheme His name and His tabernacle, *that is,* those who dwell in heaven** [heaven-dwellers, meaning believers, whether in heaven or still living in mortal bodies on earth]. <u>It was also given to him to make war with the saints and to overcome them</u> [permission given by God; *e.g.,* Job 1:12], **and <u>authority over every tribe and people and tongue and nation was given to him</u>** [by Satan, whom Jesus called **"the ruler of this world"** in **John 12:31**; see also 1 John 5:19]. **All who dwell on the earth** [earth-dwellers, meaning unbelievers] **will worship him,** *everyone* **whose name has not been written from the foundation of the world in the book of life of the Lamb who has been slain.**

2. Are the antichrist and his false prophet demon or Satan possessed?

The **dragon** we have already identified as Satan, who John previously described in **Revelation 12:3** as a **great red dragon having seven heads and ten horns, and on his heads** *were* **seven diadems.** The fact that Satan is pictured having the heads and horns of the antichrist may indicate that the antichrist is Satan-possessed; in any event he receives his authority and power from Satan.

The **beast** (antichrist) is also referred to as **the beast that comes out of the abyss**: **Revelation 11:7: When they** [the two witnesses] **have finished their testimony, <u>the beast that comes up out of the abyss</u> will make war with them, and overcome them and kill them. Revelation 17:8: The<u> beast</u> that you saw was, and is not, and <u>is about to come up out of the abyss</u> and go to destruction.** Could this indicate that the antichrist is indwelled by one of Satan's fallen angels of Genesis 6:1-4, who married women and were therefore bound and confined in **pits of darkness, reserved for judgment** according to 2 Peter 2:4 (see also Jude 6)? Scripture gives no definite answer.

The entire unholy trinity is definitely controlled by Satan, and the beast and the false prophet <u>appear</u> to be demon-possessed in **Revelation 16:13-14a: And I saw** *coming* **out of the mouth of the dragon and out of the mouth of the beast and out of the mouth of the false prophet, three unclean spirits like frogs; for they are spirits of demons....** Whether or not they are actually demon possessed, they have definitely been given supernatural demonic powers by Satan, and do his bidding without question.

3. The number 666

Revelation 13:18 tells us: **Here is wisdom. Let him who has understanding calculate the number of the beast, <u>for the number is that of a man</u>; and his number is six hundred and sixty-six.** Seven is the number of completion or perfection in the Bible. The number six falls short, indicating incompletion and mortality, in this case mankind. The three-fold repetition may indicate the certainty of that fact, a Jewish usage (*e.g.,***John 3:3: "Truly, truly, I say to you, unless one is born again he cannot see the kingdom of God."**) or may be a clue to be solved by assigning numerical value to the letters of his name, but despite many attempts, no one can say with certainty at this time what the number 666 means.

4. Satan uses the antichrist to imitate Christ.

In **Matthew 28:18, Jesus said, "All authority has been given to Me in heaven and on earth."** Satan is unable, of course, to give his antichrist any authority in heaven, but, as shown in Revelation 13:2 above, Satan gives him Satan's power and **great authority** on earth, which God has permitted, apparently since Satan's fall described above, with limitations protecting believers such as the hedge protecting Job that we see in Job 1:10. (Remember, that protection is apparently removed during the last half of the tribulation period. Rev. 13:7, Daniel 7:25). In fact, when we look at **Revelation 13:8** above, we see that [a]**ll who dwell on the earth** [unbelievers] **will worship him** during the last half of the tribulation, an obvious attempt to imitate Jesus' authority and deity during His reign in the millennial kingdom.

The antichrist even imitates Christ's death and resurrection in Revelation 13:3 (quoted above), causing **the whole earth** (of unbelievers) to worship Satan and the beast (antichrist).

5. The beast's ten horns and seven heads

But what about the beast's ten horns and seven heads and ten diadems (crowns of authority)? They are first mentioned **in Daniel 7:7-8, 11** [Daniel speaking]:
"After this I kept looking in the night visions, and behold, a fourth beast, dreadful and terrifying and extremely strong; and it had large iron teeth. It devoured and crushed and trampled down the remainder with its feet; and it was different from all the beasts that were before it, <u>and it had ten horns</u>. While I was contemplating the horns, behold, another horn [the antichrist], **a little one, came up among them, and three of the first horns were pulled out by the roots before it; and behold, this horn possessed eyes like the eyes of a man and a mouth uttering great** *boasts....*"

They are mentioned again as ten kings who have given their authority to the antichrist and are apparently subordinates ruling under him in **Revelation 17:12-14a:** [One of the seven angels who are holding the seven bowls is speaking to John in his vision] **"The ten horns which you saw are ten kings who have not yet received a kingdom, but they receive authority as kings with the beast for one hour. These have one purpose, and they give their power and authority to the beast. These will wage war against the Lamb** [Jesus] **and the Lamb will overcome them..."** [a reference to the battle of Armageddon, indicating they will reign under the antichrist until the end of the tribulation]

Daniel's description of the **fourth beast** follows a description of the first three in Daniel 7:4-6. In Daniel's vision, Babylon appears as a lion, Persia as a bear, and Greece as a leopard, indicating that the beast as described in Revelation 13:2 above has some of the characteristics of those world empires.

However, the beast (antichrist) clearly comes out of the fourth empire, the Roman empire, and not the old Roman empire, but a future one, as Daniel is told in **Daniel 7:23-25: "Thus he** ["one of those who were standing by" in his night vision (v. 16), presumably an angel] **said: 'The fourth beast will be a fourth kingdom on the earth, which will be different from all the** *other* **kingdoms and will devour the whole earth and tread it down and crush it. As for the ten horns, out of this kingdom ten kings will arise; and another** [the antichrist] **will arise after them, and he will be different from the previous ones and will subdue three kings. He will speak out against the Most High and wear down the saints of the Highest One, and he will intend to make alterations in times and in law; and they** [the saints] **will be given into his hand for a time, times, and half a time** [the last three and one-half years of the tribulation]**....'"**

6. *Where does the antichrist come from?*

We know the antichrist comes **out of the sea** (**Rev. 13:1**, above), and represents the **fourth kingdom on the earth**, apparently a revived Roman empire. What is **the sea**? The **many waters** on which the **great harlot** of **Revelation 17:1** sits are identified in **Revelation 17:15: And he** [the angel of Revelation 17:1] **said to me, "The waters on which you saw where the harlot sits, are peoples and multitudes and nations and tongues."** These waters, **the sea**, are the Gentile nations, *i.e.,* all the nations of the world except Israel, which is often called **the land**. (*e.g.,* **Zech. 13:8**)

However, since the antichrist comes out of the **fourth kingdom**, a revived or new version of the Roman empire, <u>it appears the antichrist comes from the Western world</u>, which would include western Europe and the Americas, what we call Western civilization. The **people of the prince who is to come** (antichrist) of **Daniel 9:26** were the Romans, who invaded Jerusalem and destroyed the temple in 70 A.D. Since the Romans are the antichrist's people, he definitely comes from what is left of the Roman empire, what we think of as Western civilization, possibly from Italy or Rome itself.

The antichrist apparently does not come from Africa or northern Asia (Russia): **Daniel 11:40:** [The supernatural man of Daniel 10:5, perhaps an angel, is speaking to Daniel] **"At the end time the king of the South will collide with**

him, and the king of the North will storm against him...." (Remember, in the Bible all directions are given with Israel as the reference point.) Nor does he come from what we call the Far East or Asia. **Daniel 11:44: "But rumors from the East and from the North will disturb him, and he will go forth with great wrath to destroy and annihilate many."** What part of the world is left? The Western world.

C. The false prophet

Although he is not called **the false prophet** until Revelation 16:13, this third member of the "unholy trinity" is described in **Revelation 13:11-17:**

Then I saw another beast coming up out of the earth [He is a man, like Adam]**; and he had two horns like a lamb and he spoke as a dragon. He exercises all the authority of the first beast in his presence.** [He has the same powers from Satan the antichrist has.] **And he makes the earth and those who dwell in it** [unbelievers] **to worship the first beast, whose fatal wound was healed. He performs great signs, so that he makes fire come down out of heaven to the earth in the presence of men** [which the prophets of Baal and the Asherah could not do on Mount Carmel in I Kings 18]**. And he deceives those who dwell on the earth because of the signs which it was given him to perform in the presence of the beast, telling those who dwell on the earth to make an image to the beast who had the wound of the sword and has come to life** [counterfeiting Jesus' death and resurrection. See Rev. 13:3]**. And it was given to him to give breath to the image of the beast, so that the image of the beast would even speak and cause as many as do not worship the image of the beast to be killed. And he causes all, the small and the great, and the rich and the poor, and the free men and the slaves, to be given a mark on their right hand or on their forehead, and *he provides* that no one will be able to buy or to sell, except the one who has the mark,** *either* **the name of the beast or the number of his name.** Note the counterfeiting of God's seal on the foreheads of the 144,000 in Revelation 7:3 and on the foreheads of God's bond-servants in Revelation 22:4.

During Christ's earthly reign in the millennial kingdom (the subject of a later chapter), mortal humans will see the closest thing to "heaven on earth." During the seven-year tribulation period that precedes it, and particularly during the last half of the tribulation period, mortal humans will, with the rule of these three who comprise "the unholy trinity", see the most terrible time mankind has experienced on earth, **"such as has not occurred since the beginning of the world...." Matthew 24:21** [Jesus speaking.] With Satan in charge with his "unholy trinity" and **"he who now restrains"** [thought to be the Holy Spirit] **"taken out of the way" 2 Thessalonians 2:7**, the world experiences all the misery that Satan's moral bankruptcy produces, as we will see when we examine the tribulation period in the next four chapters.

FOR REVIEW: (Cite verses for your answers.)

1. Who are the members of "the unholy trinity"? _____

2. Does the antichrist come out of Israel? _____

3. What part of the world does the antichrist apparently come from?
_____

4. What does the number 666 mean? _____

5. What do the beast's (antichrist's) ten horns represent? _____

6. Are the beast and false prophet demon or Satan possessed? _____

7. Describe some of the powers of the false prophet. _____
_____

8. What is meant by "those who dwell on the earth"? _____

9. What happens to those who do not worship the image of the beast? ____

10. What is the reason people get "the mark of the beast"? _____

11. What do the prophecies discussed in this chapter tell you about Satan's plan for mankind?
_____

12. Why did Satan set up an empire and rule the earth during the tribulation?

13. Why does Satan have the antichrist imitate Christ's death and resurrection?

14. Why does Satan want to mark "all who dwell on the earth" and how does it impact them?
_____

CHAPTER SIX
THE FIRST HALF OF THE TRIBULATION

MAIN IDEA: The tribulation is the most terrible seven-year period that the world will ever see. God's wrath is poured out on earth from heaven while a cruel dictator inspired by Satan eventually rules the whole world, persecuting and killing those who refuse to worship him. During the first half of the tribulation, the dictator (the **beast**, or antichrist) amasses power while keeping a peace treaty with many nations, including Israel. During this seven-year period, God's primary focus is once again fixed on Israel, and God sends His witnesses to Israel for the first three and one-half years.

A. WHAT IS THE TRIBULATION?

1. The tribulation is Daniel's seventieth **week**.

    Daniel 9:25-27: [The angel Gabriel speaking to Daniel] **"So you are to know and discern** *that* **from the issuing of a decree to restore and rebuild Jerusalem until Messiah the Prince** *there will be* **seven weeks and sixty-two weeks; it will be built again, with plaza and moat, even in times of distress. Then after the sixty-two weeks the Messiah will be cut off and have nothing, and the people** [Romans] **of the prince who is to come** [the antichrist] **will destroy the city and the sanctuary. And its end** *will come* **with a flood** [This happened in 70 A.D., and the flood was of Roman soldiers, not water.]**; even to the end there will be war; desolations are determined. And he** [the antichrist] **will make a firm covenant with the many** [nations, including Israel] **for one week, but in the middle of the week he will put a stop to sacrifice and grain offering** [when he breaks the peace treaty and conquers Jerusalem immediately before the tribulation midpoint]**; and on the wing of abominations** *will come* **one who makes desolate** [the antichrist]**, even until a complete destruction, one that is decreed** [by God]**, is poured out on the one who makes desolate."**

    The sixty-nine **weeks** (literally "sevens," meaning seven Jewish years of 360 days each, given here as seven plus sixty-two), according to some calculations, began with the issuing of the decree to rebuild Jerusalem issued by Artaxerxes Longimanus on March 14, 445 B.C. and ended on what appears to be the original Palm Sunday on April 6, 32 A.D., following which the Messiah, Jesus, was **cut off** (Daniel 9:26), that is, crucified.

    Daniel's seventieth **week** of seven Jewish years did not immediately follow the first sixty-nine weeks because of the intervening age of the church (discussed in the previous chapter). Let's take a look at how and why that happened.

a. God's plan for Israel was "put on hold" during entire church age.

The obvious gap between the sixty-ninth and seventieth week, now approaching 2000 years, was not foreseen by any of the Old Testament prophets. Why?

The Jews, except for a "remnant," rejected the Messiah. Paul explains in **Romans 9:30-31: What shall we say then? That Gentiles, who did not pursue righteousness, attained righteousness, even the righteousness which is by faith; but Israel, pursuing a law of righteousness, did not arrive at** *that* **law. Why? Because** *they did* **not** *pursue it* **by faith, but as though** *it were* **by works. They stumbled over the stumbling stone,...**

Because of this rejection, God's plan for Israel was "put on hold," but not abandoned. Paul tells us in **Romans 11:25-26a: For I do not want you, brethren, to be uninformed of this mystery** [The mystery, unrevealed to the Old Testament prophets, was the entire church age, which began on the day of Pentecost in Acts 2 and will continue until the church is removed (raptured) before the beginning of the seventieth week.]—**so that you will not be wise in your own estimation—that a partial hardening has happened to Israel until the fullness of the Gentiles has come in** [until the church age has ended]**; and so all Israel will be saved; just as it is written,**
  "The Deliverer will come from Zion,
  He will remove ungodliness from Jacob." (Quoting Isaiah 59:20)

Some Bible scholars think that God's plan for Israel was replaced by the church, and that the blessings promised to Israel are now to be bestowed on the church. This "replacement theology" has no basis in Scripture and contradicts God's clear promise to Israel in Isaiah 41:8-20, summarized at the end of **Isaiah 41:17: As the God of Israel I will not forsake them.** YHWH, translated **the Lord**, says in **Isaiah 44:21:**
  "Remember these things, O Jacob,
  And Israel, for you are My servant;
  I have formed you, you are My servant,
  O Israel, you will not be forgotten by Me...."

God's commitment to Israel is stated even more emphatically in **Jeremiah 31:35-37:**
  Thus says the Lord,
  Who gives the sun for light by day
  And the fixed order of the moon and the stars for light by night,
  Who stirs up the sea so that its waves roar;
  The Lord of hosts is His name:
  "If this fixed order departs
  From before Me," declares the Lord,
  "Then the offspring of Israel shall also cease
  From being a nation before Me forever."

> **Thus says the L**ORD**,**
> **"If the heavens above can be measured**
> **And the foundations of the earth searched out below,**
> **Then I will also cast off all the offspring of Israel**
> **For all that they have done," declares the L**ORD**.**

Similar promises throughout the Bible to the nation of Israel, with promises of Israel's restoration in the millennial kingdom (to be discussed in a later chapter), make it clear that <u>God's promises to Israel will be fulfilled</u>, and have <u>not</u> somehow been transferred to the church.

Daniel's seventieth **week** of seven Jewish years did not immediately follow the first sixty-nine weeks because of the intervening age of the church. Jesus' church and the entire church age, called **the time of the Gentiles** by Paul in **Romans 11:25**, was a **mystery** to the Old Testament prophets in the sense that it was not revealed to them. It occurred because of Israel's rejection of their Messiah. (Matthew 13:11; Romans 11:25).

<u>b. Daniel's seventieth **week** of seven years is the tribulation period yet to come.</u>

The seventieth **week** (seven Jewish years) of **Daniel 9:27** remains unfulfilled, telling us that the entire tribulation period will last seven years, not ending until the destruction of **the one who makes desolate**, the antichrist, who is thrown into the lake of fire at the end of the battle of Armageddon in Revelation 19:20.

<u>2. The tribulation is the terrible part of **the day of the L**ORD** foretold by the Old Testament prophets.</u>

Although the **mystery** of this present age (the time of the church, from the day of Pentecost in Acts 2 until the future rapture of the church) was not revealed to Israel through the Old Testament prophets, those prophets saw the events of Daniel's seventieth **week** and the events that followed it. For more on this point, see the previous chapter entitled "The Day of the LORD."

<u>3. The tribulation is that time foretold by Jesus in Matthew 24:9-22.</u>

Christ's warning of this time begins in **Matthew 24:9: "Then they will deliver you** [believers, since Jesus is addressing His disciples--apparently those saved after the rapture of the church, if the rapture occurs before the tribulation begins] **to tribulation,..."** After describing the tribulation midpoint, He then says of the last half of the tribulation, in **Matthew 24:21: "Then there will be a great tribulation,..."** That terrible 1260 days is the subject of a later chapter.

<u>4. The events and judgments of the first half of the tribulation are described in detail in Revelation chapters 8-9.</u>

The details of the first half of this seven-year tribulation period are given in Revelation chapters 8 and 9. In those chapters, the relevant number seems to be one-third, with one-third of the vegetation, sea, fresh water, heavens and mankind being seriously affected or destroyed. This one-third of mankind killed in Revelation 9:18 is in addition to the one-fourth killed in **the beginning of birth pangs** in Revelation 6:8.

5. Israel's peace treaty with the antichrist.

According to **Daniel 9:27**, the antichrist makes a peace treaty with many nations at the start of the seventieth week, the seven-year tribulation period. Israel is apparently one of those nations, because Jerusalem is not invaded and the antichrist does not **put a stop to sacrifice and grain offering** until right before the first half of the tribulation ends, *i.e.,* **the middle of the week**. During this first half of the tribulation, Israel has the benefit not only of the peace treaty, but of God's 144,002 witnesses, described below. There is no indication, however, that Israel is spared the judgments of Revelation 8-9.

5. The 144,000 of Revelation 7.

During the first half of the tribulation (1260 days), Israel has the benefit of the 144,000 Jews (**bondservants of our God**), 12,000 from each tribe of Israel, sealed **on their foreheads** (see **Revelation 7:3-8**) with the name of the Father and the Lamb (see **Revelation 14:1**). This appears to be the same seal that we see on the foreheads of God's **bond-servants** in **Revelation 22:4**.

These 144,000 serve as God's light in the world to witness, preaching the gospel presumably primarily to the nation of Israel, since they are from the twelve tribes of Israel and are all in Jerusalem at the tribulation midpoint (see Revelation 14:1). The seal is given for their protection. For example, after the fifth trumpet, the supernatural (demonic?) locusts with stings like scorpions are commanded to torment **only the men who do not have the seal of God on their foreheads** [*i.e.,* the 144,000]. **Revelation 9:4b.** Although one-third of mankind is killed after the sixth trumpet is sounded (Revelation 9:15), all 144,000 appear at the tribulation midpoint in Revelation 14:1.

Their protection during the last one-half of the tribulation period is not specified, but there is no reason to believe their protection does not continue during that time. It seems likely that they are among **those who are in Judea (Matthew 24:16**), who flee at the tribulation midpoint under God's protection, discussed in a Chapter 8.

We are all familiar with the mark of the blood of the lamb on the doorposts and lintels (the horizontal board over the doorframe) to spare the lives of the firstborns of the children of Israel in Exodus 12:7. Most of us are not so familiar with God putting His mark of protection on people's foreheads, as we see here. However, this is not the first time God uses a mark on the foreheads of those He wants to spare. We aren't told whether the sign God appointed for Cain's protection in Genesis 4:15 is a visible mark, and if so, whether it is on his forehead, but we do see God telling an angelic being to mark the foreheads of those He wants to spare in Ezekiel 9:4-7. That mark is literally a *taw*, the last letter of the Hebrew alphabet, which was written in Ezekiel's time in the shape of a cross! Remember, Ezekiel lived and wrote hundreds of years before the Romans started using crucifixion as a means of execution.

The seal of God on the foreheads of the 144,000 is described as follows in **Revelation 14:1b: one hundred and forty-four thousand, having His** [Christ's] **name and the name of His Father written on their foreheads.**

6. The two witnesses of Revelation 11.

The 144,000 "bondservants of God" (Revelation 7:3) appear to be peaceful messengers of God, spreading the salvation message in a world and a nation (Israel) filled with unbelievers. On the other hand, the two witnesses described in Revelation 11 are not so gentle.

They are described in **Revelation 11:3-6:** [The **someone** (apparently Christ) of **Revelation 11:1** is speaking.] **"And I will grant *authority* to my two witnesses, and they will prophesy for twelve hundred and sixty days** [3 ½ Jewish years of 360 days each, the first half of the tribulation], **clothed in sackcloth."**
These are the two olive trees and the two lampstands that stand before the LORD of the earth. And if anyone wants to harm them, fire flows out of their mouth and devours their enemies; so if anyone wants to harm them, he must be killed in this way. These have the power to shut up the sky, so that rain will not fall during the days of their prophesying; and they have power over the waters to turn them into blood, and to strike the earth with every plague, as often as they desire.

There has been much speculation over the identity of these two witnesses. Remember, the two witnesses must be mortals to be killed in Revelation 11:7. Certainly they are God's witnesses, and the reference to the olive trees and lampstands is almost identical to the description of Joshua and Zerubbabel that Zechariah describes in **Zechariah 4:2-3: He** [the angel] **said to me** [Zechariah] **"What do you see?" And I said "I see, and behold, a lampstand all of gold with its bowl on the top of it, its seven lamps on it with seven spouts belonging to each of the lamps which are on the top of it; also two olive trees by it, one on the right side of the bowl and the other on its left side."**

We are told in Zechariah 4:12 that golden olive oil flows from the two olive trees to keep the lamps burning, an apparent reference to the fact that Joshua and Zerubbabel are powered by the Holy Spirit (represented by the olive oil flowing from the two olive trees into the bowl on top of the lampstand), as are the two witnesses of Revelation 11. The Holy Spirit provides the light (the gospel) through the two witness, who are called **the two lampstands**.

The powers they have closely resemble the powers given to Elijah in 1 Kings 17:1 and Moses in Exodus 7:14-12:29, leading some to speculate that they are the two witnesses of Revelation 11. However, such a conclusion would have to include the concept that Elijah and Moses were either reincarnated as mortals, resurrected as mortals (Moses), or returned to earth in mortal form (Elijah apparently never died; see 2 Kings 2:11). None of these concepts has any Biblical support.

That being said, God is omnipotent, and it would be foolish to say that God cannot use Elijah and Moses for this purpose if it is His wish to do so. However, the identity of the two witnesses is not revealed, and there is no reason to believe that they are not mortal believers who are selected for this specific purpose and not taken up in the rapture of the church, or who become Christians after the rapture of church and are subsequently empowered by God in Revelation 11:3.

These two witnesses appear to center their ministry in Jerusalem, where their bodies lie in the street after the antichrist kills them in Revelation 11:7: **Revelation 11:8: And their dead bodies *will lie* in the street of the great city which mystically is called Sodom and Egypt, where also their Lord was crucified.**

The unbelieving world looks at the bodies (Some think this a prediction of television and 24/7 cable news.) and celebrates their death with a Christmas-like celebration, where they **send gifts to one another**, while the two bodies lie in the street for three and one-half days. Then we read in **Revelation 11:11: But after the three and a half days, the breath of life from God came into them, and they stood on their feet; and a great fear fell upon those who were watching them. And they heard a loud voice from heaven saying to them, "Come up here." Then they went up into heaven in the cloud, and their enemies watched them.**

After the death, resurrection and ascension of the two witnesses, we read in **Revelation 11:15a: Then the seventh angel sounded** [the seventh trumpet], indicating the end of the first half of the tribulation, thus placing the ministry of the two witnesses in the first half of the tribulation and the breaking of the peace treaty (the invasion of Israel by the antichrist) immediately before the end of the first half of the tribulation. Their death at the hands of the antichrist coincides with his invasion of Jerusalem **in the middle of the week** as described in Daniel 9:27 above, and spoken of by Jesus in **Matthew 24:15-16:**
"Therefore when you see the ABOMINATION OF DESOLATION which was spoken of through Daniel the prophet, standing in the holy place [the temple in Jerusalem, apparently rebuilt before the end of the first half of the tribulation]**...then those who are in Judea must flee to the mountains...."**

Jesus is speaking here of the **middle of the week** of Daniel 9:27, which brings us to the tribulation midpoint, the subject of a later chapter.

FOR REVIEW: (Cite verses for your answers)

1. What is the tribulation? _____

2. How long does it last? _____

3. Who described it using the word "tribulation"? _____

4. What is "replacement theology"? _____

5. Does God ever abandon Israel? _____

6. Describe the 144,000 witnesses. _____

7. What seal do the 144,000 witnesses have? _____

8. Where and when do the two witnesses die? _____

9. What powers do the two witnesses have? _____

10. What is God's purpose for the two witnesses? _____

10. Is Israel ruled by the antichrist during the first half of the tribulation? _____
_____

11. What do the prophesied events discussed in this chapter tell you about the character of God?
_____
_____

12. Do you think you will be living on earth during this time? _____

13. Why do you think God has the two witnesses killed and then resurrected and taken to heaven?
_____

14. What do you think happens to the 144,000 witnesses? _____
_____

CHAPTER SEVEN
BABYLON THE GREAT

MAIN IDEA: Revelation 17 describes BABYLON THE GREAT as a harlot, an international religious organization which is hostile toward God and kills Christians. Revelation 18 calls the woman "the great city," representing a world-wide corrupt economic system. Both are destroyed, apparently at the tribulation midpoint, paving the way for all political, religious and economic power to be concentrated in Satan's earthly representative, the antichrist, during the last half of the tribulation period.

Revelation chapters 17 and 18 describe the judgment (destruction) of **BABYON THE GREAT** [**Rev. 17:5**]. These chapters are anything but clear, and have therefore been the subject of much discussion and disagreement among Bible scholars, but some conclusions can be reached with reasonable certainty.

1. John's Vision of the Great Harlot in Revelation 17

Revelation 17:1-6: Then one of the seven angels who had the seven bowls came and spoke with me, saying, "Come here, I will show you the judgment of the great harlot who sits on many waters, with whom the kings of the earth committed *acts of* immorality, and those who dwell on the earth were made drunk with the wine of her immorality." And he carried me away in the Spirit into a wilderness; and I saw a woman sitting on a scarlet beast, full of blasphemous names, having seven heads and ten horns. The woman was clothed in purple and scarlet, and adorned with gold and precious stones and pearls, having in her hand a gold cup full of abominations and of the unclean things of her immorality, and on her forehead a name was written, a mystery, "BABYLON THE GREAT, THE MOTHER OF HARLOTS AND OF THE ABOMINATIONS OF THE EARTH." And I saw the woman drunk with the blood of the saints, and with the blood of the witnesses of Jesus. When I saw her, I wondered greatly.

2. The Angel's Explanation of the Vision

After explaining that the beast on which the woman is sitting is the antichrist, the angel tells John, **"Here is the mind which has wisdom. The seven heads are seven mountains on which the woman sits; …. The woman whom you saw is the great city, which reigns over the kings of the earth." Revelation 17:9,18.** We saw her name written on her forehead as **BABYLON THE GREAT** in verse 5, and now she is identified with **the great city**, and as sitting on seven mountains, all of which clearly ties her to Rome, at the same time identifying Rome as the antichrist's center of power. Babylon was commonly used as a code name for Rome in the first century to avoid conflict with the Roman authorities. *See* *e.g.* 1 Peter 5:13.

Whether Rome stands for the actual city in Italy or the Western center of world power when the antichrist assumes power in the Western world is unclear, but Rome itself is indicated here. So whatever the woman represents is centered either in Rome itself, or Rome is being used as representative of the seat of power in the Western world during the time of the tribulation, as it was the actual seat of power when Revelation was written.

But exactly what does the woman represent? She is seen on the back of the beast, which represents the antichrist, in verse 3, suggesting that her power and influence is somehow tied to that part of the Western world controlled by the antichrist. Later we see that the ten kings and the beast (representing the consolidated political power under the antichrist) [the angel of Revelation 17:1 is speaking] " ...**will hate the harlot and will make her desolate and naked, and will eat her flesh and will burn her up with fire...." Revelation 17:16b.** She therefore does not represent political power, and is in fact destroyed by the political power headed by the antichrist.

Revelation 17:15: And he [the angel] **said to me, "The waters which you saw where the harlot sits, are peoples and multitudes and nations and tongues."** The woman represents a widespread organization involving multitudes of people from many nations, apparently covering much of the same territory in the Western world ruled by the antichrist when he receives authority from the ten kings, since she is seen sitting on the beast.

The first clue to the nature of this organization comes in verse one, where the angel calls her **the great harlot**, and having **THE MOTHER OF HARLOTS** written on her forehead in verse five. We know this is how God views unfaithfulness to Him. We see it over and over again in the writings of the prophets. It is the theme of the entire book of Hosea, which begins: **When the LORD first spoke through Hosea, the LORD said to Hosea, "Go, take to yourself a wife of harlotry and have children of harlotry; for the land commits flagrant harlotry, forsaking the LORD." Hosea 1:2.** The same language appears in Judges, when Israel forsakes the LORD and worships other gods. For examples, see Judges 2:17, 8;27,33.

In **Revelation 17:2** quoted above, we see that **"those who dwell on the earth** [unbelievers] **were made drunk with the wine of her immorality."** But this is not just an international organization of unbelievers engaging in immoral behavior and turning away from God. We see the woman in **Revelation 17:6b drunk with the blood of the saints, with the blood of the witnesses of Jesus.** This is an international organization with the blood of believers on its hands, an active enemy of God. The only type of organization with that kind of scope and power (that does not have controlling political power) that comes to mind is some type religious organization. This conclusion also explains why she is called a **harlot**, indicating apostasy, *i.e.,* turning away from God. There is no point in speculating about whether this organization or religion currently exists. All Scripture tells us is that it will exist during the first half of the tribulation.

The obvious question is, if this is a widespread religious organization hostile to God that engages in all sorts of immorality and even kills believers, why would Satan's chosen political leaders, the antichrist and his ten kings, destroy it? It appears to be a very effective tool for Satan. However, Satan and his political henchmen may see its destruction as necessary to pave the way for the world-wide worship of the image of the beast described in Revelation 13:15. Nevertheless, the real reason is given in **Revelation 17:17a:** [the angel of Revelation 17:1 is speaking] **"For God has put it in their hearts to execute His purpose...."** Satan thinks he is doing what he wants to do, but, just like Nebuchadnezzar when he conquered Jerusalem, he is really doing what God wants him to do.

3. The Woman as the Great City in Revelation 18

The angel who explained to John the mystery of the woman in Revelation 17 immediately gives another explanation at the end of that chapter: **"The woman whom you saw is the great city, which reigns over the kings of the earth." Revelation 17:18.** Now the woman represents something else, not the international religious organization of Revelation 17, although the description in Revelation 18:3 sounds a lot like Revelation 17:2. The difference comes in what is added to the end of Revelation 18:3, which is absent in Revelation 17:2: **"...and the merchants of the earth have become rich by the wealth of her sensuality." Revelation 18:3b.**

In addition to being a place full of demons and unclean spirits (v.2), the **great city** is also the world commercial center, with a huge shipping center (v. 17-19), existing under Satan's world system and corrupt even to the point in trading in **slaves and human lives**. (v.13). The end of the **great city**, which apparently represents the world's economic system in Revelation 18, is announced in **Isaiah 21:9 and Revelation 18:2: "Fallen, fallen is Babylon...,"** and is described by the voice of Revelation 18:4 [apparently Christ] in **Revelation 18:8: "For this reason in one day her plagues will come, pestilence and mourning and famine, and she will be burned up with fire; for the Lord God who judges her is strong."** In verses 10 and 17 the same "voice" says that **"in one hour such great wealth has been laid waste!" Revelation 18:17.**

How can the economy and wealth of the entire world be **laid waste** in one hour? Our God is a God of infinite resources and unlimited power. As the angel Gabriel told Mary, **"For nothing will be impossible with God." Luke 1:38.** Many possibilities comes to mind that are not that difficult to foresee at this time. One that fits the narrative of the activities of the unholy trinity: the collapse of the major world currency at the time, to pave the way for the antichrist's control of all economic activity with the mark of the beast, discussed in the previous chapter.

A collapse of the world monetary system would certainly trigger the loss of wealth described Revelation 18:9-19, and would usher in the antichrist's replacement of the monetary system: the mark of the beast to buy and sell, described in **Revelation 13:16-17: And he** [the false prophet] **causes all, the small and the great, and the rich and the poor, and the free men and the slaves, to be given a mark on their right hand or on their forehead., and** *he provides* **that no one will be able to buy or to sell, except the one who has the mark,** *either* **the name of the beast, or the number of his name.**

Such a system is not hard to understand in the information age, with things like barcodes and computer chip implants, and would be an obvious replacement in the case of a currency collapse. However, while Revelation chapter 18 certainly describes a collapse of the world's economic system, whether it is actually speaking of a collapse of the world's monetary system is unclear.

4. The Timing Question

The next question then becomes, **"when will these things happen?" Matthew 24:3b.** Although not clear, they probably take place either before or very shortly after the antichrist achieves world domination, sometime around the tribulation midpoint. We see the following announcement at the tribulation midpoint in **Revelation 14:8: And another angel, a second one, followed, saying, "Fallen, fallen is Babylon the great, she who has made all the nations drink of the wine of the passion of her immorality."**

This timing fits with the worship of the image of the beast and the requirement of the mark of the beast to buy and sell during the last three and one half years of the tribulation when the antichrist exercises world domination. (Daniel 7:25; Revelation 13:5), making it probable that Revelation 14:8 refers to the destruction of both the world religious system and the world economic system, apparently around the midpoint of the tribulation. The result is unlimited power in the antichrist, representing the Satanic forces of unbridled evil, and abject misery for most of mankind for three and one-half years, the subject of a later chapter.

FOR REVIEW: (Cite verses for your answers.)

1. What does the woman on the beast represent in Revelation 17? _____

2. What happens to the woman of Revelation 17? _____

3. What does the woman represent in Revelation 18? _____

4. What happens to the "great city" in Revelation 18? _____

5. When are the woman of Revelation 17 and the "great city" of Revelation 18 destroyed?
_____

6. What will be the result of the destruction of the woman called BABYLON THE GREAT of Revelation 17?
_____

7. What will be the result of the destruction of the woman called BABYLON THE GREAT of Revelation 18?

_____

CHAPTER EIGHT
THE TRIBULATION MIDPOINT

MAIN IDEA: At the tribulation midpoint, (1) there is war in heaven and Satan and his fallen angels no longer have access to heaven, (2) an angel preaches the gospel to the whole world, and (3) Christ returns to earth, splitting the Mount of Olives to make a wide valley so believers in Jerusalem and Judea can escape the invasion of the antichrist by fleeing east to the wilderness, where they are protected by God during the last half of the tribulation.

A number of very significant events occur at the midpoint of the tribulation, many of which have been ignored or misunderstood by most commentaries. <u>Readers who have read commentaries on end times prophecies are encouraged to put aside their preconceptions and take a fresh look at the Scriptures.</u>

Revelation chapters 12 and 14 describe events occurring at the tribulation midpoint, with the description of the unholy trinity sandwiched in between in chapter 13, possibly because the impact of the unholy trinity on Israel is not great until the antichrist conquers Jerusalem at the end of the first half of the tribulation period. Remember, after the rapture of the church, God's focus, as it was prior to the cross, is fixed on Israel.

A. <u>War in Heaven</u>

Revelation 12:7-10: And there was war in heaven, Michael and his angels waging war with the dragon. The dragon and his angels waged war, and they were not strong enough, and there was no longer a place found for them in heaven. And the great dragon was thrown down, the serpent of old who is called the devil and Satan, who deceives the whole world; he was thrown down to the earth, and his angels were thrown down with him. Then I heard a loud voice in heaven, saying, "Now the salvation, and the power, and the kingdom of our God and the authority of His Christ have come, for the accuser of our brethren has been thrown down, <u>he who accuses them before our God</u> day and night.

Although thrown down to earth after Satan's rebellion against God (before his appearance in the Garden of Eden) and no longer permitted to dwell in heaven (see Ezekiel 28:16-17), Satan and his fallen angels have had continual <u>access</u> to heaven and the throne of God (see Job 1:6-7) until losing this battle at the tribulation midpoint. Until this battle, Satan still has direct access to the very throne of God, as the underlined portion of the quotation above shows us. Satan and his fallen angels being thrown down to earth and no longer having access to heaven may be good news for believers in heaven, but it's not so good for believing mortals on earth, as we will see in Chapter 9 and when we examine the last half of the tribulation period.

B. The Flight of Israel

Revelation 12:1,6: A great sign appeared in heaven: a woman clothed with the sun, and the moon under her feet, and on her head a crown of twelve stars [a clear reference to Israel, see Genesis 37:9]**;.... Then the woman fled into the wilderness where she had a place prepared by God, so that there she would be nourished for one thousand two hundred and sixty days** [three and one-half years of 360 days each by the Jewish calendar].

Revelation 12:12b [spoken by "a loud voice in heaven." Revelation 12:10a] **.... "Woe to the earth and the sea, because the devil has come down to you, having great wrath, knowing that he has *only* a short time."** This woe is the third of the three woes coming to unbelievers announced in Revelation 8:13, and the repercussions on earth are immediate: **Revelation 12:13-17: And when the dragon saw that he was thrown down to the earth, he persecuted the woman** [Israel- Rev. 12:1, quoted above] **who gave birth to the male *child*** [Jesus]. **But the two wings of the great eagle** [identified as God in Revelation 12:6 above; see also Exodus 19:4] **were given to the woman, <u>so that she could fly into the wilderness</u> to her place, where she was nourished for a time and times and half a time,** [three and one-half years] **from the presence of the serpent** [Satan]. Here we see the woman, identified as Israel in Revelation 12:1-2,5, fleeing from the advancing army of the antichrist under the protection of God.

This tribulation midpoint flight of the nation of Israel at the invasion by the antichrist was described by Jesus in **Matthew 24: 15-16: "Therefore when you see the ABOMINATION OF DESOLATION which was spoken through Daniel the prophet, standing in the holy place (let the reader understand)** [*i.e.,* Jesus is quoting Daniel 9:27] **then those who are in Judea must flee to the mountains;...."** Note that flight does not commence <u>until the antichrist has already invaded Jerusalem and desecrated the temple</u>. This fits with the timing of the antichrist killing the two witnesses of Revelation 11 in Jerusalem three and one-half days <u>before</u> the seventh trumpet sounds in Revelation 11:15, ending the first half of the tribulation.

"[T]he mountains" Jesus refers to in Matthew 24:16 are east of Jerusalem and Judea, in present-day Jordan, land described to Daniel by a heavenly being, apparently an angel, in **Daniel 11:41: "He** [the antichrist] **will also enter the Beautiful Land** [Israel]**, and many *countries* will fall; but these will be rescued out of his hand: Edom; Moab and the foremost of the sons of Ammon."** These three ancient nations constitute the land across the Jordan east of Judea and Jerusalem, containing Bozrah, thought to be southeast of the Dead Sea and possibly including the ancient abandoned city of Petra, where **"those who are in Judea" "flee to the mountains."** God will apparently preserve this land from the antichrist as a place to protect **"those who are in Judea"** from the antichrist and Satan during the last three and one-half years of the tribulation period

(Revelation 12:6, 14).

However, the flight and the preservation of this place of refuge is not without peril, bloodshed and supernatural intervention. The LORD [YHWH, Jesus] tells Zechariah in **Zechariah 14:2-5: "For I will gather all the nations against Jerusalem to battle and the city will be captured, the houses plundered, the women ravished and half of the city exiled, but the rest of the people will not be cut off from the city. Then the LORD** [Jesus, by Himself] **will go forth and fight against those nations, as when He fights on a day of battle. In that day His feet will stand on the Mount of Olives, which is in front of Jerusalem on the east; and the Mount of Olives will be split in its middle from east to west by a very large valley, so that half of the mountain will move toward the north and the other half toward the south. You** ["those who are in Judea" in Matthew 24:16] <u>**will flee by the valley of My mountains**</u>**, for the valley of the mountains will reach to Azel; yes, you will flee just as you fled before the earthquake in the days of Uzziah king of Judah.** <u>**Then**</u> [at a later time] **the LORD, my God, will come,** *and* <u>**all the holy ones with Him**</u>**!"**

We see here that Jesus' descent to and splitting of the Mount of Olives (a wide mountain just across the Kidron valley east of Jerusalem) is for the <u>express purpose</u> of preparing a valley for "those who are in Judea" to flee toward the mountains to the east. Such a flight only occurs at the tribulation midpoint, and therefore places the timing of this event at the tribulation midpoint, and not at the end of the tribulation as is commonly assumed. The battle of Armageddon takes place away from Jerusalem, and there is no indication in Revelation 19 or elsewhere that Jerusalem is captured immediately prior to that battle. Also note that the passage above ends with an emphasis on the fact that this is <u>not</u> the "second coming," when He returns to rule (the subject of a later chapter). **"Then the LORD, my God, will come, and all the holy ones with Him."(v. 5b)**

At this tribulation midpoint appearance to split the Mount of Olives, the LORD comes <u>alone</u>, while at His appearance in Revelation 19, (universally acknowledged as a description of His "second coming") we read in **Revelation 19:14: And** <u>**the armies**</u> **which are in heaven, clothed in fine linen, white and clean,** <u>**were following Him**</u> **on white horses.**

We do know that when Jesus returns to rule three and one-half years later in Revelation 19:11-16 at the battle of Armageddon (the "second coming"), his robe appears **dipped in blood**. We are told in **Revelation 19:13a:** *He is* **clothed with a robe dipped in blood.** And we are told in **Revelation 19:15b: He treads the wine press of the fierce wrath of God, the Almighty.** So where does He get the blood on his robe, and what is this **winepress of the fierce wrath of God, the Almighty**? The answers appear to be given in **Isaiah 63:1-8:**
> **Who is this who comes from Edom,** [where Bozrah is located]
> **With garments of glowing colors from Bozrah,**
> **This One who is majestic in His apparel,**
> **Marching in the greatness of His strength?**

"It is I [Jesus] who speak in righteousness, mighty to save."
Why is Your apparel red,
And Your garments like the one who treads in the wine press?
"I have trodden the wine trough alone,
And from the peoples there was no man with Me.
I also trod them in My anger
And **trampled them in My wrath;**
And **their lifeblood is sprinkled on My garments,**
And I stained all My raiment.
For the day of vengeance was in My heart,
And My year of redemption has come.
I looked, and there was no one to help,
And I was astonished and there was no one to uphold;
So My own arm brought salvation to Me,
And My wrath upheld Me.
I trod down the peoples in My anger
And made them drunk in My wrath,
And I poured out their lifeblood on the earth."

The **lifeblood** poured out on the earth is further described by John in his details on the tribulation midpoint given in Revelation chapters 12 and 14. We read in **Revelation 14:17-20: And another angel came out of the temple which is in heaven, and he also had a sharp sickle. Then another angel, the one who has power over fire, came out from the alter; and he called with a loud voice to him who had the sharp sickle, saying, "Put in your sharp sickle and gather the clusters from the vine of the earth, because her grapes are ripe." So the angel swung his sickle to the earth and gathered** *the clusters from* **the vine of the earth, and threw them into the great wine press of the wrath of God. And the wine press was trodden outside the city, and blood came out from the wine press, up to the horses' bridles, for a distance of two hundred miles.**

The actual distance should be translated one hundred eighty miles, and appears to refer to a winding flight to and through mountains east of Jerusalem going south to Bozrah, perhaps Petra, but the place in the wilderness where God protects **the woman** is only identified as Bozrah in Isaiah 63:1-8.

The distance, the reference to the wine press, God's (Jesus') wrath, and the placement of this description in Revelation at the tribulation midpoint all indicate that this passage refers to the battle or series of battles taking place during the flight at the midpoint of the tribulation, and not the final battle of Armageddon as is commonly assumed.

Another passage which seems to refer to this slaughter and bloodshed, describing it in terms of a great animal sacrifice, is found in **Isaiah 34:5-8:**
For My sword is satiated in heaven,
Behold it shall descend for judgment upon Edom
And upon the people whom I have devoted to destruction.

**The sword of the LORD is filled with blood,
It is sated with fat, with the blood of lambs and goats,
With the fat of the kidneys of rams,
For the LORD has a sacrifice in <u>Bozrah</u>
And a great slaughter in the land of Edom.
Wild oxen shall also fall with them
And young bulls with strong ones;
<u>Thus their land shall be soaked with blood,</u>
And their dust become greasy with fat.
<u>For the LORD has a day of vengeance,</u>
A year of recompense for the cause of Zion.**

Reviewing what we have seen so far on the flight of Israel, we have:

(1) God keeps the mountain area east of the Jordan River out of the hands of the antichrist (Daniel 11:41), apparently preserving it as a place of refuge (Revelation 12:6,14) for those fleeing Jerusalem and Judea at the tribulation midpoint (Matthew 24:16).

(2) Immediately before the tribulation midpoint, the middle of Daniel's seventieth week of seven years in Daniel 9:27, the antichrist breaks his treaty, invades Israel and conquers Jerusalem (Daniel 11:41, Matthew 24:16, Zechariah 14:2).

(3) Jesus, who has warned of the invasion and the necessity for flight in Matthew 24:16, makes a path of escape to the east by descending to earth at the Mount of Olives and splitting it in the middle to make a large valley east of Jerusalem so the inhabitants can flee east to the mountains (Zechariah 14:4-5).

(4) A fierce battle or series of battles ensues during the flight, in which Jesus Himself participates, apparently all the way from Jerusalem to Bozrah (Zechariah 14:1-8). This battle leaves a trail of blood one hundred eighty miles, apparently a winding trail from Jerusalem, first going east through the valley created by Jesus' splitting of the Mount of Olives, across the Jordan River, then south on the east side of the Jordan River through the mountains all the way to Bozrah (Revelation 14:20, Isaiah 34:5-8;63:1-8, all quoted above).

(5) Those fleeing Judea and Jerusalem are protected by God (apparently YHWH, the LORD, *i.e.,* Jesus) **in the wilderness**, *i.e.,* Bozrah, thought to be the area including the ancient abandoned city of Petra, for the last half of the tribulation period (Revelation 12:6,14).

So who are those fleeing Jerusalem and Judea under God's protection? They are only referred to in Revelation 12 as **the woman** who is clearly identified as the nation of Israel, but many think God will only be rescuing the believing "remnant" out of the clutches of the antichrist. If the heavenly being who appears to Daniel in Daniel 10:5-6 is speaking of the tribulation midpoint in Daniel 12:1, those fleeing are in fact only the believing Jewish remnant: **Daniel 12:1: "Now at that time Michael, the great prince who stands *guard* over the sons of your people, will arise. And there will be a time of distress such as never occurred since there was a nation until that time** [words Jesus echoed in Matthew 24:21, indicating that Daniel 12:1 is indeed speaking of a time immediately preceding the start of the last half of the tribulation]**; and at that time <u>your people</u>** [Israel]**,**

everyone who is found written in the book, will be rescued."

The "book" is God's book of life containing the names of all believers, mentioned in Revelation 17:8, making those fleeing believers. This view fits with the general theme of the tribulation, in which God's wrath is directed at unbelievers, and with God's preservation of the believing remnant of Israel throughout history. (Incidentally, Michael's role in end time events is unrevealed except for this reference and his role in the war in heaven described in Revelation 12:7-9.)

Those Jewish believers fleeing under God's protection could include the 144,000 witnesses sealed by God in Revelation 7. The last mention of them is at the tribulation midpoint, when John sees them with Jesus on Mount Zion (Jerusalem) in **Revelation 14:1: Then I looked, and behold, the Lamb *was* standing on Mount Zion, and with Him one hundred and forty-four thousand, having His name and the name of His Father written on their foreheads.** The fact that they are all gathered in Jerusalem with Jesus and are never mentioned again, plus the fact that God's protection of believers under the rule of the antichrist is apparently removed during the last half of the tribulation, while God protects all 144,000 during the first half of the tribulation, all indicate they may be among those protected by God in **the wilderness** during the last half of the tribulation. (Revelation 12:6, 14)

While God's wrath is directed at unbelievers, note that after the believing Jewish remnant from Jerusalem and Judea is rescued, Satan's wrath is directed at the remaining believers on earth. Let's take another look at **Revelation 12:17: So the dragon was enraged with the woman, and went off to make war with the rest of her children, who keep the commandments of God and hold to the testimony of Jesus.** All believers are Abraham's spiritual descendants, the heirs to the promise of God (Galatians 3:26-29), and here are called **the rest of her children**.

C. The Gospel Preached to the Whole World

While the exact timing sequence of all the events occurring at the midpoint of the tribulation are unclear, Jesus in **Matthew 24:14** refers first to the preaching of the gospel **"in the whole world for a witness to all the nations, and then the end will come."** To the extent that the gospel has not been preached to all the nations before the tribulation midpoint, it appears to take place in **Revelation 14:6-7: And I saw another angel flying in midheaven, having an eternal gospel to preach to those who live on the earth** [earth-dwellers, *i.e.*, unbelievers], **and to every nation and tribe and tongue and people; and he said with a loud voice, "Fear God, and give Him glory, because the hour of His judgment has come; worship Him who made the heaven and the earth and sea and springs of waters."**

D. The Big Picture on the Tribulation Midpoint

Immediately prior to the tribulation midpoint, the antichrist breaks his treaty with the many nations not yet under his control and invades Jerusalem (Daniel 9:27; Revelation 11:7). Meanwhile, in heaven, Satan and his fallen angels lose a war to Michael and his angels, and are thrown out of heaven and no longer have access to heaven and the throne of God (Revelation 12:7-11). Enraged, Satan intensifies his persecution of believers on earth during the remaining three and one-half years of the tribulation (Revelation 12:13, 17).

Jesus (by Himself) descends to earth and splits the Mount of Olives to make a valley for believers in Jerusalem and Judea to flee east across the Jordan to **the wilderness** (apparently Bozrah, thought to be the area southeast of the Dead Sea). Jesus protects this believing remnant of Israel during a bloody battle or series of battles, and God, probably also Jesus, protects them in **the wilderness** for the last half of the tribulation period (Revelation 12:6,14).

After an angel **flying in midheaven** preaches the gospel to the whole world of unbelievers in **Revelation 14:6-7** (fulfilling Jesus' words of Matthew 24:14), the stage is set for what Jesus called **a great tribulation** in **Matthew 24:21**, the subject of our next chapter.

FOR REVIEW: (Cite verses for your answers.)

1. At what time during the tribulation will Jerusalem be invaded and captured?

2. Why does Jesus descend to earth and split the Mount of Olives? _____

3. Who flees "into the wilderness"? _____

4. What happens to those who flee into the wilderness during the second half of the tribulation?

5. When are Satan and his fallen angels thrown out of (and no longer have access to) heaven?

6. How is the gospel "preached to the whole world" at the tribulation midpoint?

7. Why is Jesus' apparel red in Isaiah 63? _____

8. Where are the 144,000 witnesses when they are last mentioned?

_____

9. What does Satan do after losing the war in heaven? _____

_____

10. What place is mentioned as a possible place where those who flee into the wilderness are protected during the last half of the tribulation? _____

11. List the differences between the battle described in Zechariah 14 and the battle of Armageddon in Revelation 19.

_____

_____

12. What do the prophesied events described in this chapter tell us about God's promises?

_____

CHAPTER NINE
THE LAST HALF OF THE TRIBULATION

MAIN IDEA: At the end of the first half of the tribulation, the antichrist breaks his peace treaty and invades Israel, eventually conquering the entire world. The international religious organization and the world's economic system have both been destroyed, and the antichrist seizes control of both, thereby concentrating all political, religious, and economic power in his hands. God's protection for believers on the earth is apparently removed as the antichrist's persecution intensifies, while God's seven "bowl" judgments are rained down upon the earth.

The antichrist's military campaign and conquests are detailed in the words of the supernatural messenger sent to Daniel in **Daniel 11:40-44: "....At the end time the king of the South will collide with him** [the antichrist]**, and the king of the North will storm against him with chariots, with horsemen and with many ships; and he will enter countries, overflow** *them* **and pass through. He will also enter the Beautiful Land** [Israel]**, and many** *countries* **will fall; but these will be rescued out of his hand: Edom, Moab and the foremost of the sons of Ammon. Then he will stretch out his hand against** *other* **countries, and the land of Egypt will not escape. But he will gain control over the hidden treasures of gold and silver and over all the precious things of Egypt; and Libyans and Ethiopians** *will follow* **at his heels. But rumors from the East and from the North will disturb him, and he will go forth with great wrath to destroy and annihilate many...."**

How far does his conquest go? We learn in **Rev. 13:5b, 7** that **authority to act for forty-two months was given to him....It was also given to him to make war with the saints and to overcome them, and authority over every tribe and people and tongue and nation was given to him.** The answer appears to be: The antichrist rules the entire world during the last half of the tribulation, except for the **wilderness** east of the Jordan which God keeps **out of his hand** [Daniel 11:41] as a place for God to protect **those who are in Judea** who **flee to the mountains**. (Matthew 24:16; Revelation 12:6,14)

Note that <u>God's protection for the saints appears to be removed during this terrible time</u> (see Daniel 7:25 quoted below and Rev. 13:7, quoted above), <u>even as Satan's war against them intensifies:</u> **Rev. 12:17: So the dragon was enraged with the woman** [the believing remnant of Israel, see the chapter on the tribulation midpoint]**, and went off to make war with the rest of her children, who keep the commandments of God and hold to the testimony of Jesus** [believers, Abrahams' spiritual descendants, see Galatians 3:7].

What does this war on the saints look like? We are told in **Rev. 13:15-17: And it was given to him** [the false prophet, the antichrist's lieutenant, the third member of the unholy trinity] **to give breath to the image of the beast** [the antichrist], **so that the image of the beast would even speak and <u>cause as many as do not worship the image of the beast to be killed</u>. And he causes all, the small and the great, and the rich and the poor, and the free men and the slaves, to be given a mark on their right hand or on their forehead, and** *he provides* **that <u>no one will be able to buy or to sell, except the one who has the mark</u>,** *either* **the name of the beast or the number of his name.**

Apparently, all believers will have to be in hiding (to avoid being seen <u>not</u> worshiping the image of the beast, and <u>not</u> having the mark of the beast on their right hand or forehead). Furthermore, they will have to resort to an underground barter economy to get enough food to survive.

Daniel's friends, who we remember by their Babylonian names of Shadrack, Meshach and Abed-nego, confronted a similar problem in Daniel 3 (required worship of an image) and Daniel together with those same three dealt with a food problem (the problem of being required to eat the unclean food from the king's table) in Daniel 1:8-21. They overcame both problems and prospered, but in both instances they had God's help and protection, which apparently will not be available to believers during these three and one-half years.

While Satan is persecuting and killing believers, unbelievers (those **who dwell on the earth—Rev. 13:8**), are dealing with God's wrath being poured out of the bowls on the earth as described in Revelation 16: **loathsome and malignant sore**[s] (v.2) on all unbelievers who had received the mark of the beast and had worshiped his image (first bowl); sea turning to something like blood and killing everything in the sea (second bowl); fresh water turning to blood (third bowl); scorching heat (fourth bowl); darkness (fifth bowl); Euphrates river dried up (sixth bowl); massive geophysical upheavals, with a great earthquake destroying cities, nations, islands and mountains, followed by one hundred pound hailstones (seventh bowl).

Revelation chapters 17 and 18 detail the destruction of Satan's world-wide religious and commercial establishments, apparently near the tribulation midpoint. These chapters dealing with the destruction of **Babylon the great (Rev.14:8)** were discussed in an earlier chapter, and are mentioned here as a reminder of how terrible a time this three and one-half years will be. After dealing with Satan's world-wide religious system, which makes war on and kills the saints during the first half of the tribulation, believers will find themselves trying to survive in a world where the economic system has just been destroyed, and with it much of the world's wealth.

And they must do this without worshipping the image of the beast or receiving his mark in this last half of the Tribulation. There is reason to believe that many will also starve, given the combination of economic collapse and the requirement of receiving the mark of the beast to buy or sell.

To make matters worse, as noted above, God's protection of believers during this time appears to be removed, and many believers are probably martyred during this period: **Daniel 7:25: He** [the antichrist] **will speak out against the Most High and wear down the saints of the highest One, and he will intend to make alterations in times and in law; and <u>they</u>** [the saints] <u>**will be given into his hand**</u> **for a time, times, and half a time** [the last three and one-half years of the tribulation]. **Revelation 13:7a: It was also given to him** [the antichrist] **to make war with the saints and to overcome them,...**

So what happens if one who considers himself a believer, perhaps to save his family from starving to death, receives the mark of the beast so he can buy food? The answer is given in **Revelation 14:9-11: Then another angel, a third one, followed them, saying with a loud voice, "If anyone worships the beast and his image, and receives a mark on his forehead or on his hand, he also will drink of the wine of the wrath of God, which is mixed in full strength in the cup of His anger; and <u>he will be tormented with fire and brimstone</u> in the presence of the holy angels and in the presence of the Lamb. And the smoke of their torment goes up <u>forever and ever</u>; they have no rest day and night, those who worship the beast and his image, and whoever receives the mark of his name."**

The message is clear: [Jesus speaking] **"No servant can serve two masters...." Luke 16:13.** Even giving outward "lip service" to the beast by receiving his mark will result in condemnation. Jesus, addressing His twelve disciples in Matthew 10, put it this way:

Matthew 10:22: "You will be hated by all because of My name, but it is the one who has endured to the end who will be saved."

Matthew 10:28: "Do not fear those who kill the body but are unable to kill the soul; but rather fear Him who is able to destroy both soul and body in hell."

Matthew 10:32-33: "Therefore everyone who confesses Me before men, I will also confess him before My Father who is in heaven. But whoever denies Me before men, I will also deny him before My Father who is in heaven."

Paul gave the same message to the Corinthians in **1 Corinthians 15:1-2a: Now I make known to you, brethren, the gospel which I preached to you, which also you received, in which also you stand, <u>by which also you are saved, if you hold fast the word which I preached to you</u>....** See also Colossians 1:21-23.

One final quotation from **Revelation 12:10-11:** [A loud voice in heaven speaking] **"Now the salvation, and the power, and the kingdom of our God and the authority of His Christ have come, for the accuser of our brethren has been thrown down, he who accuses them before our God day and night. And they overcame him because of the blood of the Lamb and because of the word of their testimony, <u>and they did not love their life</u>**

even when faced with death." (See also Colossians 1:21-23.)

Are you prepared to die for your faith? If not, is it sufficient to meet the faith God requires for salvation? Remember, your faith is a gift from God, not of your own doing (Ephesians 2:8-9). If you have any doubt about your faith, remember the cry of the father of the demon-possessed boy to Jesus in **Mark 9:24: "I do believe; help my unbelief."**

The events of Revelation chapters 17 and 18 concentrate worldwide political, religious and economic power in the antichrist, even as God continues to pour out His judgments on the earth, making the last half of the tribulation a terrible time for both believers and unbelievers who have survived to this point. How terrible? Jesus called it **"a great tribulation, such as has not occurred since the beginning of the world until now, nor ever will." Matthew 24:21.**

Jesus then said in **Matthew 24:22: "Unless those days had been cut short, no life would have been saved; but for the sake of the elect those days will be cut short."** How are they cut short? By His return to rule, the subject of a later chapter.

FOR REVIEW: (Cite verses for your answers.)

1. What part of the world does the antichrist control during the last half of the tribulation?
_____

2. What two bad things happen to believers during the second half of the tribulation?
_____

3. What will people be required to do in order to buy food during the second half of the tribulation?
_____

4. What happens to everyone who receives the mark of the beast? _____
_____

5. According to Jesus, what happens to people who deny Him before men?
_____

6. Who does Jesus say we should fear? _____

7. What do the events prophesied in this chapter tell us about God's position toward those who reject His gift of salvation?
_____

CHAPTER TEN
THE JUDGMENT SEAT OF CHRIST

MAIN IDEA: After death or rapture and before Christ's return at the battle of Armageddon at the end of the tribulation, all Christians will appear before Christ to receive rewards for all they have allowed God to do through them while "abiding in Christ."

In the previous chapters we have been examining what will happen on earth during the terrible seven-year period we call the tribulation. Our focus now changes to heaven, as Christians appear before what Paul calls **"the judgment seat of Christ**." **2 Cor. 5:10**, quoted below.

Most Christians are aware that one day they will face judgment, but many are vague on the details: "Does this judgment determine whether I spend eternity in heaven or hell?" "Why must I be judged, if Christ paid for my sins on the cross and I am redeemed?" If I am saved by faith, not works, why must my works be judged?" "What will be the result of this judgment?" This chapter will examine some of the passages in Scripture which refer to this judgment, and hopefully answer some of these concerns.

Romans 14:10,12: But you, why do you judge [Gr. *krisis*-condemn] **your brother** [fellow believer]**? Or you again, why do you regard your brother with contempt? For <u>we will all stand before the judgment seat</u>** [*bema*] **<u>of God</u>....So then each one of us will give an account of himself to God.**

Note that Paul is clearly writing to and about believers, those indwelled with the Holy Spirit. He also writes to believers in **2 Corinthians 5:10: For we must all appear before the judgment seat of Christ, so that each one may be recompensated for his deeds in the body, according to what he has done, whether good or bad** [*kakos*]**.**

The judgment seat of Christ (God), then, is only for believers. Unbelievers are judged at the great white throne judgment, discussed in Chapter 15. This judgment does not concern the issue of salvation, for only the saved will appear there. When we look at the two passages above, we see the purpose of our giving an account is for the purpose of recompensation, or reward, not for the purpose of examining believers' past sins.

The idea that this is not an examination of believers' sins is borne out by the Greek word used, *bema*, meaning "judgment seat" or "throne." It connotes no indication of condemnation. By contrast, the word **judged** in **John 3:18** is the word *krino* in the Greek, from the root word *krisis,* meaning accusation, condemnation, damnation or judgment. A variation of the same Greek word *krisis* is translated **judged (Revelation 20:12)** at the great white throne judgment, resulting in all unbelievers being condemned to the lake of fire. Since the word *bema* is used to refer to this judgment, instead of the word *krisis* or *krino*, the implication is that there will be no condemnation of any kind at this judgment, only rewards.

The description of the deeds in 2 Corinthians 5:10 as "good or bad" raises the same question. What do "good" and "bad" mean in this context, and how do they affect the reward each believer will receive when judged? We find a clue but no definitive answer in **1 Corinthians 3:11-16: For no man can lay a foundation other than the one which is laid, which is Jesus Christ. Now if any man builds on the foundation with gold, silver, precious stones, wood, hay, straw, each man's work will become evident; for the day** [of judgment] **will show it because it is *to be* revealed with fire, and the fire itself will test the quality of each man's work. If any man's work which he has built on it remains, he will *receive* a reward. If any man's work is burned up, he will suffer loss; but he himself will be saved, yet so as through fire. Do you not know that you are a temple of God and *that* the Spirit of God dwells in you?**

The last sentence indicates that only believers will appear at this judgment.

The **wood, hay, straw** are the "bad" works of 2 Corinthians 5:10. The Amplified Bible (1965 ed.) translates the word "evil" instead of "bad," while the Holman Christian Study Bible (2010 ed.) translates the word "worthless" instead of "bad." If the **wood, hay, straw** which is "burned up" is "evil," then it represents sin and the believer's sins are weighted against his **gold, silver, precious stones** to determine if his "good works" outweigh his sins for the purpose of determining whether **he will *receive* a reward**. If the **wood, hay, straw** are "worthless," they represent "good works" done in the flesh, which merit no favor with God, and therefore are **burned up** at this judgment, are then gone, and count for nothing.

The latter interpretation seems to fit with Jesus' statement in **John 15:4-5: "Abide in Me, and I in you. As the branch cannot bear fruit of itself unless it abides in the vine, so neither *can you* unless you abide in Me. I am the vine, you are the branches; he who abides in Me and I in him, he bears much fruit, <u>for apart from me you can do nothing</u>."** If the fruit is the **gold, silver, precious stones** representing the works honored (and therefore rewarded), the **gold, silver, precious stones** must be the works done "in the Spirit" as opposed to those done in the flesh, which apparently are **nothing** before God, *i.e.,* have no lasting value, and are therefore **burned up** because they are worthless, which seems to be a better interpretation of the Greek word *kakos*.

In **Isaiah 26:12,** the prophet quotes part of a song of praise that will be sung by believers in the millennial kingdom (to be discussed in a later chapter):
"LORD, You will establish peace for us,
Since <u>You have also performed for us all our works</u>."

These verses indicate that the only works God values (and therefore rewards) are <u>the works believers allow God to do through them by being controlled by the Spirit</u> instead of by the flesh. How is this done? See Galatians 5:16-25 and 1

John 1:9.

There is another reason to interpret the word "bad" as "worthless" instead of "evil." Many passages in the Old and New Testaments say that God will not remember believers' sins. **Hebrews 10:17:** (quoting Jeremiah 31:34)

> "AND THEIR SINS AND THEIR LAWLESS DEEDS
> I WILL REMEMBER NO MORE."

See Isaiah 38:17 and 43:25 for similar passages. Logically, this makes sense. Since Christ died for all the sins of the world, past, present and future, sin is no longer the issue in the spiritual realm, although it certainly is in the earthly realm, where it has earthly consequences (See Hebrews 12:6). If God puts our sins behind His back (Isaiah 38:17) and remembers them no more, there is no reason for God to remind us of them and judge them at this judgment, which is solely for the purpose of rewarding believers, not humiliating them. Believers should look forward to meeting Jesus and undergoing this judgment with joy and gratefulness, not fear.

The judgment results in **a reward** for every believer whose work survives the fire. This reward appears to take the form of crowns of honor or recognition (Gr. *Stephanos*), not crowns of authority (Gr. *Diadems)*. Some of these crowns are described in the following verses: 1 Corinthians 9:24-25 (imperishable wreath); 1 Thessalonians 2:19 (crown of exultation); 2 Timothy 4:7-8 (crown of righteousness); James 1:12 (crown of life); 1 Peter 5:4 (crown of glory).

Exactly when this judgment will take place is not clear, although it will certainly take place for all believers who are part of the church <u>before</u> Christ returns to earth for the final battle of Armageddon at the end of the Tribulation. Speaking of the church, the bride of the Lamb (the subject of the next chapter), John writes in **Revelation 19:8: It was given to her to clothe herself in fine linen, bright *and* clean; for <u>the fine linen is the righteous acts of the saints</u>.** <u>The cloth for the wedding dress comes from this judgment.</u> Heaven opens and Christ appears three verses later, placing this judgment before Christ's return.

These **righteous acts** cannot be determined until the **wood, hay, straw** have been **burned up** and only the **gold, silver, precious stones** remain, indicating the judgment seat of Christ has already taken place for all these believers <u>before</u> the bride of Christ appears in Revelation 19:8. It seems probable, <u>but is by no means clear</u> (*e.g.* 1 Peter 5:4), that believers will be judged at the moment they meet their Savior, be it by means of death, or rapture in the case of believers alive in their mortal bodies when the rapture occurs. **For now we see in a mirror dimly, <u>but then face to face</u>; now I know in part, but then I will know fully just as I also have been fully known. 1 Corinthians 13:12**

Every believer should look forward to meeting his Savior with joyful anticipation of receiving rewards and welcome, not condemnation. Until then, we do well to seek to be controlled by the Spirit and have God do His work through us, instead of striving to do works for Him in the flesh. Not only is it easier, more joyful and more fulfilling, it will also be more rewarding when we meet Him at this judgment.

FOR REVIEW: (Cite verses for your answers.)

1. Who appears at the judgment seat of Christ? _____

2. What is the significance of the judgment seat being called the *bema*?
_____

3. What is the reason a person has to appear at the judgment seat of Christ?
_____

4. When does a person appear at the judgment seat of Christ? _____
_____

5. Name some of the crowns awarded at the judgment seat of Christ. _____
_____

6. Are you looking forward to the judgment seat of Christ? Why or why not?
_____

CHAPTER ELEVEN
THE MARRIAGE OF THE LAMB

MAIN IDEA: The New Testament church is the bride of Christ, and Revelation 19 talks of an actual wedding ceremony and wedding supper. This chapter discusses when and where the marriage and the marriage supper take place and identifies the invited guests.

A. <u>The Marriage</u>

The final revealed event that takes place in heaven before Jesus returns to conquer and rule on the earth is His marriage, announced shortly before the battle of Armageddon (variously spelled Armagedon and Har-Magedon in different translations). The scene <u>in heaven</u> is described in **Revelation 19:6-7: Then I heard** *something* **like the voice of a great multitude and like the sound of many waters and like the sound of mighty peals of thunder, saying, "Hallelujah! For the Lord our God, the Almighty, reigns. Let us rejoice and be glad and give the glory to Him, for <u>the marriage of the Lamb has come</u> and His bride has made herself ready."**

So exactly who is this bride, and when and where does this marriage and marriage supper take place? And who are the invited guests?

The answer to the first question is given in **Ephesians 5:25-27: Husbands, love your wives, just as Christ also loved the church and gave Himself up for her, so that He might sanctify her, having cleansed her by the washing of water with the word, that He might present to Himself the church in all her glory, having no spot or wrinkle or any such thing; but that she would be holy and blameless.** Writing to the church at Corinth, Paul said in **2 Corinthians 11:2: For I am jealous for you with a godly jealousy; for I betrothed you to one husband, so that to Christ I might present you** *as* **a virgin.**

The bride of Christ is the church, that is, the body of believers living from the day of Pentecost described in Acts 2 (when the time of the church began with the filling of the apostles with the Holy Spirit) to the rapture of the church, when the entire church, the living and dead, is transformed into immortal bodies and removed from earth as described in 1 Corinthians 15: 51-57 (quoted in Chapter 4). Elsewhere in Scripture, both Israel (*e.g.,* Hosea 2:19-20) and the new Jerusalem (Revelation 21:2) are spoken of as brides, perhaps of Christ, but in this passage and in Revelation 19, the bride of the Lamb is clearly the church.

As to the timing question, the marriage cannot take place before the rapture of the church has occurred as described in 1 Corinthians 15:51-57. Otherwise, the church would be neither complete nor in immortal (glorified) bodies. Since this announcement that **His bride has made herself ready (Rev. 19:7)** is given <u>in</u>

<u>heaven and</u> <u>before</u> Christ's return to earth as the King at the battle of Armageddon, it gives us additional evidence that the rapture of the church occurs before His return to rule.

Furthermore, the marriage will take place <u>after</u> the judgment seat of Christ occurs, in which Christ separates the **wood, hay, stubble** from the **gold, silver, precious stones** (1 Corinthians 3:10-15). The **gold, silver, precious stones** <u>are</u> the **righteous acts of the saints** which must be determined beforehand, since the **righteous acts of the saints** is the material for the wedding gown: **Revelation 19:8: It was given to her** [the bride] **to clothe herself in fine linen, bright *and* clean; for** <u>**the fine linen is the righteous acts of the saints.**</u>

The marriage appears to take place in heaven, the home of the bride (the church). **Philippians 3:20: For our citizenship is in heaven, from which also we eagerly wait for a Savior, the Lord Jesus Christ;.... 1 Thessalonians 4:17: Then we who are alive and remain will be caught up** [raptured] **together with them** [the resurrected believers who are part of the church] **in the clouds to meet the Lord in the air, <u>and so we shall always be with the Lord.</u>** (See chapter 4). See also Philippians 1:23.

B. <u>The Marriage Supper</u>

The marriage appears to be the like the traditional two part Jewish marriage, where the husband (some time after the marriage contract between the bride's father and the groom--this time is called the betrothal period) first goes to the house of the bride to pay the bride's father the agreed contract amount and consummate the marriage. The wedding couple then goes to the groom's house for the marriage supper and celebration, where the guests are invited.

In Revelation 19:8, quoted above, the marriage ceremony itself appears to be about to take place or to have already taken place in heaven, at the home of the bride, since the focus shifts in verse 9 to the marriage supper, which comes after the wedding ceremony, just as we have the reception dinner after the marriage ceremony in traditional marriages today: **Revelation 19:9: Then he** [the voice from the throne in Revelation 19:5] **said to me, "Write, 'Blessed are those who are invited to the marriage supper of the Lamb.'" And he said to me, "These are true words of God."**

The timing and location of the marriage supper, and the answer to the question of who are the invited guests, are both suggested in the parable of the ten virgins in Matthew 25:1-13, discussed in the next chapter. In that parable, Christ is the bridegroom, and the ten virgins are waiting for the appearance of the bridegroom to go in with Him to the marriage feast. Since the bridegroom is Christ, the ten virgins awaiting His return are apparently professing mortal believers living on earth at the time of His return. The five virgins (believers) with oil (representing the Holy Spirit) are admitted to the wedding feast, while the five without the oil (unbelievers) are shut out.

Earth represents the home of the bridegroom, where Christ is coming to rule His kingdom for the next 1000 years. We see from this parable that the guests invited to the wedding feast include the mortal true believers alive at the time of Christ's return. The guests logically also include all deceased believers not part of the church, to be resurrected in glorified bodies at the time of His return, as discussed in the next chapter. These guests in glorified immortal bodies would include all Old Testament saints and all tribulation saints killed during the seven-year tribulation period.

In short, it is reasonable to assume that <u>all</u> believers will be at the marriage supper of the Lamb, either in their glorified, immortal bodies or in their mortal state (in the case of believers surviving the tribulation), and that <u>this supper takes place on earth after all uninvited guests (*i.e.,* unbelievers) are removed</u> at the judgments taking place at His return. This would place the timing for the marriage supper at the start of Christ's reign, the millennial kingdom, discussed in chapter 13. It will truly be a time of great joy and celebration as all believers from all ages, both mortals and immortals, are united for the first time at one of the most significant events ever to occur on earth!

There are significant implications of being the bride of Christ for those of us who are members of the church. We know that God, *i.e.,* Christ, is an all powerful, all knowing, truthful, loving person who has eternal life. And He will be that way forever. **Malachi 3:6a: "For I, the LORD, do not change...." Hebrews 13:8: Jesus Christ is the same yesterday and today and forever.**

Think about it. This caring, loving God Who suffered greatly and died in agony so that we might spend eternity with Him will treat us as a perfect husband would treat his bride. We can expect Him to continue to love us with His love that passes our understanding, to continue to provide for us in every way, and continue to protect us through all eternity. That's the promise He makes to the church when He agrees to make us His bride.

FOR REVIEW: (Cite verses for your answers.)

1. Who or what is the bride of Christ? _____

2. What are the benefits of being the bride of Christ? _____
_____

3. Where does the marriage ceremony of Christ and His bride take place? _____
_____

4. Where does the wedding feast of the marriage of the Lamb take place? _____
_____

5. Who will be the guests at the wedding feast? _____

6. Will the ten virgins be guests at the wedding feast? _____
_____

7. When does the wedding feast of the marriage of the Lamb take place?_____
_____

CHAPTER TWELVE
CHRIST RETURNS TO RULE

MAIN IDEA: Christ's return to earth (a) begins with His appearance at the battle of Armageddon, and is followed by (b) the battle of Armageddon, (c) His regathering of the nation of Israel, (d) the resurrection of all Old Testament and deceased tribulation saints in their immortal bodies, and (e) His judgment of all living mortals. In that judgment, all unbelieving mortals are killed, leaving only believing mortals to enter the millennial kingdom together with Christ and all saints from every age in their glorified immortal bodies.

Christ's return to conquer, regather the nation of Israel, judge, and rule is described in many Old and New Testament passages. Numerous events occur at or immediately after this "second coming," and are discussed below. Events clearly occurring or continuing after His return are the subjects of later chapters. Each significant event is discussed in a separate section, as follows:

1. HIS APPEARANCE
2. ARMAGEDDON
3. THE REGATHERING OF THE NATION OF ISRAEL
    A. The Mortals Who Survive the Tribulation
    B. Resurrection of the Jewish Old Testament Saints
4. RESURRECTION OF THE OLD TESTAMENT GENTILE SAINTS AND THE TRIBULATION SAINTS
5. THE JUDGMENTS
    A. Israel Judged
    B. The Basis for Judgment Explained
    C. The Judgment of the Nations (Gentiles)
6. THE BIG PICTURE

1. HIS APPEARANCE

Isaiah 13: 9-10:
Behold, <u>the day of the LORD is coming</u>,
Cruel, with fury and burning anger,
To make the land a desolation;
And <u>He will exterminate its sinners from it</u>.
For the stars of heaven and their constellations
Will not flash forth their light;
<u>The sun will be dark when it rises</u>
<u>And the moon will not shed its light</u>.

After describing the destruction of the antichrist in Daniel 7:11, Daniel writes in **Daniel 7:13-14:**
I kept looking in the night visions,

> **And behold, <u>with the clouds of heaven</u>**
> **<u>One like a Son of Man was coming</u>,**
> **And He came up to the Ancient of Days**
> **And was presented before Him.**
> **And to Him was given dominion,**
> **Glory and a kingdom,**
> **That all the peoples, nations and** *men of every* **language**
> **Might serve Him.**
> **His dominion is an everlasting dominion**
> **Which will not pass away;**
> **And His kingdom is one**
> **Which will not be destroyed.**

Jesus apparently refers to these passages (and others, *e.g.,* Joel chapter 2) when He prophesies of His return in **Matthew 24:29-30**: "But <u>immediately after the tribulation</u> of those days THE SUN WILL BE DARKENED, AND THE MOON WILL NOT GIVE ITS LIGHT, AND THE STARS WILL FALL from the sky, and the powers of the heavens will be shaken. And then the sign of the Son of Man will appear in the sky, and then all the tribes of the earth will mourn, and they will see the SON OF MAN COMING ON THE CLOUDS OF THE SKY with power and great glory."

So Jesus Himself tells us that He will return **immediately** after the **tribulation....** Earlier in the same discourse, He speaks of **a great tribulation** in Matthew 24:22: "Unless those days had been cut short, no life would have been saved; but for the sake of the elect those days will be cut short." He cuts those days (the second half of the tribulation) short by His return as the conquering King.

John describes His return in **Revelation 19:11-16:**

> And I saw heaven opened, and behold, a white horse, and He who sat on it is called Faithful and True, and in righteousness He judges and wages war. His eyes *are* a flame of fire, and on His head are many diadems and He has a name written *on Him* which no one knows except Himself. He is clothed with a robe dipped in blood, and His name is called The Word of God. And the armies which are in heaven, clothed in fine linen, white *and* clean, were following Him on white horses. From His mouth comes a sharp sword, so that with it He may strike the nations, and He will rule them with a rod of iron; and He treads the wine press of the fierce wrath of God the Almighty. And on His robe and on His thigh He has a name written, "KING OF KINGS, AND LORD OF LORDS."

2. ARMAGEDDON

Most people in the Western world, believers and unbelievers, understand Armageddon to be the final battle between good and evil at the end of the world. Except for the fact that this "battle" is not much of a battle, is not the end of the world, and is not even the final battle between good and evil, God and Satan, this view would be correct.

According to **Revelation 12:7-12**, at the tribulation midpoint, the dragon (Satan) and his angels lose the war in heaven against the archangel Michael and his angels, and are literally **thrown down to the earth** (v.9), and no longer have access to heaven and the throne of God (v.10) (See Section A of Chapter Eight). Nevertheless, Satan, **knowing that he has *only* a short time** (v.12), prepares for a rematch on earth, this time using men as additional troops.

The gathering of Satan's forces for this epic battle is described in **Revelation 16:12-14, 16: The sixth *angel* poured out his bowl on the great river, the Euphrates; and its water was dried up, so that the way would be prepared for the kings from the east. And I saw *coming* out of the mouth of the dragon and out of the mouth of the beast and out of the mouth of the false prophet, three unclean spirits like frogs; for they are spirits of demons, performing signs, which go out to the kings of the whole world, to gather them together for the war of the great day of God, the Almighty.... And they gathered them together, to the place which in Hebrew is called Har-Magedon** [called Armagedon and Armageddon in other translations].

The Hebrew word Armageddon may mean "hill of Megiddo," which would place the battle on or near the plain of Megiddo, in northwest Israel, southwest of Nazareth and the Sea of Galilee. In any event, it is not the same battle as the one in which the antichrist conquers Jerusalem at the tribulation midpoint.

The stage is set, and the "battle," to use the term loosely, is described in **Revelation 19:19-21: And I saw the beast and the kings of the earth and their armies assembled to make war against Him who sat on the horse and against His army. And the beast was seized, and with him the false prophet who performed the signs in his presence, by which he deceived those who had received the mark of the beast and those who worshiped his image; these two were thrown alive into the lake of fire which burns with brimstone. And the rest were killed with the sword which came from the mouth of Him who sat on the horse, and all the birds were filled with their flesh.**

That's it. No contest. Satan and his angels and all the armies of the earth are no match for God's overwhelming power over His creation. **1 John 4:4b: ...greater is He who is in you than he who is in the world.**

John's vision shows the beast (antichrist) and the false prophet (his lieutenant) being thrown alive into the lake of fire, while we read in **Daniel 7:11:**

"Then I kept looking because of the sound of the boastful words which the horn was speaking. I kept looking until the beast was slain, and its body was destroyed and given to the burning fire."

So will the mortal body of the beast (and presumably the false prophet) be killed and then thrown into the lake of fire, or thrown alive into the lake of fire as John wrote? Although not clear, it seems likely that both accounts are correct. That is, their mortal bodies will be killed, and immediately transformed into their immortal bodies that will feel torment but not be destroyed by the lake of fire, where they will be thrown, making them the lake's first revealed inhabitants, and the only unbelievers who do not appear at the great white throne judgment (discussed in Chapter 15).

This is the second death, spiritual death, to be discussed later. If they are thrown alive in their mortal bodies into the lake of fire, those mortal bodies will be immediately consumed, and presumably their souls would then go to the place of torment (in Hades, *i.e.,* the underworld) described by Jesus in Luke 16:23-24. The implication in both accounts, however, is that the beast and the false prophet will have reached their final destination, implying that they are in immortal bodies that will not be destroyed by the fire, but will be tormented forever.

The final event we see at the end of this battle is the imprisonment of Satan and his angels in the abyss for one thousand years, removing all demonic influence from the earth during Christ's reign in what we call the millennium, and the Old Testament prophets and Jesus called **the kingdom of God** or **the kingdom of heaven** (See, *e.g.* John 3:3.): **Revelation 20:1-3: Then I saw an angel coming down from heaven, holding the key of the abyss and a great chain in his hand. And he laid hold of the dragon, the serpent of old, who is the devil and Satan, and bound him for a thousand years; and he threw him into the abyss, and shut** *it* **and sealed** *it* **over him, so that he would not deceive the nations any longer, until the thousand years were completed; after these things he must be released for a short time.** [Satan and his angels are released at the end of the millennium to fight the battle of Gog and Magog.]

> **Isaiah 14:15:**
> **Nevertheless you** [Satan] **will be thrust down to Sheol,**
> **To the recesses of the pit.**

This tells us about Satan; what about his angels? Apparently they are thrown in the abyss also.

> **Isaiah 24:21-22:**
> **So it will happen in that day** [the day of the LORD]
> **That the LORD will punish the host of heaven on high,** [Satan's angels]
> **And the kings of the earth on earth.**
> **They will be gathered together**
> **Like prisoners in the dungeon**

**And will be confined in prison;
And after many days they will be punished.**

3. THE REGATHERING OF THE NATION OF ISRAEL

A. The Mortals Who Survive the Tribulation

The regathering of the nation of Israel for entrance into the Kingdom of God is one of the most prophesied events in the Old Testament. Examples can be found in Deuteronomy 30:1-5, Isaiah 27:12-13, Ezekiel 37:1-28, and Zechariah 10:8-10. One passage giving a full picture is **Ezekiel 20:33-38: "As I live," declares the Lord GOD** [Jesus]**, "surely with a mighty hand and with an outstretched arm and with wrath poured out, I shall be king over you. <u>I shall bring you out from the peoples and gather you from the lands where you are scattered</u>, with a mighty hand and with an outstretched arm and with wrath poured out; and I shall bring you into the wilderness of the peoples, and there I shall enter into judgment with you face to face. As I entered into judgment with your fathers in the wilderness of the land of Egypt, so I will enter into judgment with you," declares the Lord GOD. "I shall make you pass under the rod, and I shall bring you into the bond of the covenant; and <u>I shall purge from you the rebels and those who transgress against Me</u>; I shall bring them out of the land where they sojourn, <u>but they will not enter the land of Israel.</u> Thus you will know that I am the LORD."**

All of the living descendants of the nation of Israel will be regathered from all over the globe and placed **in the wilderness of the peoples** (v.35), presumably east of the Jordan, where the people of Israel wandered for forty years. Their subsequent judgment (**I shall purge from you the rebels** (v.38)) will be discussed in Section E below.

This regathering of the nation of Israel is described by Jesus in His Olivet discourse: **Matthew 24:31: "And He will send forth His angels with A GREAT TRUMPET** [See Zech. 9:14b, Isaiah 27:12-13] **and THEY WILL GATHER TOGETHER His elect** [Israel] **from the four winds, from one end of the sky to the other."**

Some of you may be thinking the "elect" can only mean believers whose names were written in the Lamb's book of life before the foundation of the world (Revelation 13:8b). But the context does not support that interpretation. It cannot mean the church, because the church has already been gathered at the rapture and is in heaven at this point. From the moment of the rapture of the church, God's attention is focused on His "elect," His chosen people, the nation of Israel.

His chosen people, His "elect" always has been and always will be the nation of Israel, and that is His meaning here, which lines up with all the Old Testament prophecies concerning the regathering of the nation of Israel at His return to rule in His Kingdom. (See Isaiah 27:12-13.) (We Gentile believers, also known as "the elect," have been spiritually "grafted in" to share in the promises God made to the nation of Israel--as to salvation, but to what extent in the millennial kingdom is unspecified; see Romans 11:17-24.)

B. The Jewish Old Testament Saints

The Jewish Old Testament saints (believers) will be resurrected in immortal (glorified) bodies, regathered and placed in the land of Israel. In a poem of praise and prophecy, Isaiah says to the LORD, in **Isaiah 26:19:**
Your [the LORD'S] **dead will live;**
Their corpses will rise.

Isaiah continues, addressing the dead bodies of Israel's believers:
You who lie in the dust, awake and shout for joy,
For your dew is as the dew of the dawn,
And the earth will give birth to the departed spirits.

After Ezekiel sees a vision of God raising a whole valley full of dead bones, and giving them life as **an exceedingly great army** (Ezek. 37:10), God tells him in **Ezekiel 37: 12-14: "Therefore prophesy and say to them** [the house of Israel], **'Thus says the Lord GOD, "Behold, <u>I will open your graves and cause you to come up out of your graves</u>, <u>my people</u>; <u>and I will bring you into the land of Israel</u>. Then you will know that I am the LORD, when I have opened your graves and caused you to come up out of your graves, <u>My people.</u> I will put My Spirit within you and <u>you will come to life, and I will place you on your own land.</u>"...'"**

This resurrection of Israel's dead will be for believers only. Of the unbelieving dead, Isaiah says in **Isaiah 26:14:**
The dead will not live, the departed spirits will not rise;
Therefore You have punished and destroyed them.
And You have wiped out all remembrance of them.

As we will see, the unbelieving dead will finally be resurrected one thousand years later, to appear at the great white throne judgment.

4. RESURRECTION OF THE OLD TESTAMENT GENTILE SAINTS AND THE TRIBULATION SAINTS

The Gentile Old Testament saints are, like the New Testament Gentile saints, also **grafted in** to the nation of Israel (Romans 11:19), **heirs according to promise** made to Abraham (Galatians 3:29), and are therefore resurrected at this time. John tells us in Revelation 20:6 that this is part of the first resurrection, *i.e.,* the resurrection of the saints in immortal bodies to an eternity with God, of which Jesus is the **first fruits**. **I Corinthians 15:20-23: But now Christ has been raised from the dead, the first fruits of those who are asleep. For since by a man *came* death, by a man also *came* the resurrection of the dead. For as in Adam all die, so also in Christ all will be made alive. But each in his own order: Christ, the first fruits, after that <u>those who are Christ's at His coming</u>.**

Job 19:25-27a [Job speaking]:
"**As for me, I know that my Redeemer lives,
And <u>at the last He will take
His stand on the earth</u>.
Even after my skin is destroyed,
Yet <u>from my flesh I shall see God</u>;
Whom I myself shall behold,
And whom my eyes shall see and not another.**"

Job apparently lived in the patriarchal age, perhaps around the time of Abraham, about 2000 B.C. He was certainly an Old Testament saint. There is nothing in the book of Job to connect him with the nation of Israel, which may not have even existed at the time he lived, so he was probably a Gentile. Yet he <u>knows</u> that when Jesus comes to **take His stand on the earth,** *i.e.,* rule, he (Job) will see Him from his resurrected body. There is no reason to believe that what is true for Job is not true for all the Old Testament Gentile saints.

Following a description of the martyred tribulation period saints, we read in **Revelation 20:4b: ... and they came to life and reigned with Christ for a thousand years.** The deceased tribulation saints will be there in their resurrected, immortal glorified bodies.

The church, composed of all believers, both Jewish and Gentile, will also be there in the glorified, immortal bodies received at the moment of the rapture, appearing as the bride of Christ, as we will see in the next chapter.

The Scriptures indicate that <u>all</u> believers from every age will enter the millennial kingdom, either as mortals (believers surviving the tribulation), or in their resurrected, immortal bodies.

5. THE JUDGMENTS

In His Olivet discourse, Jesus describes the judgments that will take place on His return, in which all mortal unbelievers are removed from the earth and sent to eternal punishment. **Matthew 24:37-41: "For the coming of the Son of Man will be just like the days of Noah. For as in those days before the flood they were eating and drinking, marrying and giving in marriage, until the day that Noah entered the ark, and they did not understand until the flood came and took them** [the unbelievers] **all away; so will the coming of the Son of Man be. Then there will be two men in the field; one** [the unbeliever] **will be taken and one will be left. Two women** *will be* **grinding at the mill; one** [the unbeliever] **will be taken and one will be left."**

Many people think this passage refers to the rapture, when believers are taken, and unbelievers are left. However, in His explanation of the parable of the wheat and tares, Jesus explains that it is the <u>unbelievers</u> who are taken at His return to rule:

Matthew 13:37-42: And He said, "The one who sows the good seed is the Son of Man, and the field is the world; and *as for* the good seed, these are the sons of the kingdom and the tares are the sons of the evil *one*; and the enemy who sowed them is the devil, and the harvest is the end of the age; and the reapers are angels. So just as the tares are gathered up and burned with fire, so shall it be at the end of the age. The Son of Man will send forth His angels, and they will gather out of His kingdom all stumbling blocks, and those who commit lawlessness, and will throw them into the furnace of fire; in that place there will be weeping and gnashing of teeth."

The same message is given by Jesus again in **Matthew 13:47-50: "Again, the kingdom of heaven is like a dragnet cast into the sea, and gathering *fish* of every kind; and when it was filled, they drew it up on the beach; and they sat down and gathered the good *fish* into containers, but the bad they threw away. So it will be at the end of the age; the angels will come forth and take out the wicked from among the righteous, and will throw them into the furnace of fire; in that place there will be weeping and gnashing of teeth.**

Looking back at Matthew 24:37-41, we see that Jesus is saying that, just as in the days of Noah, when all the unbelievers were removed from the earth (drowned), they will be removed (killed) when He returns to set up His kingdom, leaving only believers to enter the (millennial) kingdom. Why? Jesus gave Nicodemus the answer in **John 3:3: "Truly, truly, I say to you, unless one is born again he cannot see the kingdom of God."** All unbelievers must be removed to prepare the earth for the millennial kingdom.

A. Israel Judged.

Take another look at what Jesus says in the passage from Ezekiel 20:33-38 quoted in Section 3(A) above. We see that the regathering is followed by a judgment in **the wilderness**, in which Jesus **purges** the **rebels** and **those who transgress** against Him (*i.e.,* the unbelievers), and they do not enter the land of Israel.

Isaiah 13:9:
    Behold, the day of the LORD is coming,
    Cruel, with fury and burning anger,
    To make the land [Israel] **a desolation** [the last half of the tribulation];
    And He will exterminate its sinners from it [at His return].

Many commentators think the parable of the ten virgins refers to this judgment of the Jews at His return. It certainly refers to this *time* of judgment and to His dividing believers from unbelievers, and removing the unbelieving mortals from the earth, leaving only believing mortals alive to enter the millennial kingdom. The parable begins in **Matthew 25:1-2: "Then the kingdom of heaven** [*i.e.*, the judgment of mortals at His return to determine who will remain to enter the kingdom as mortals and who are killed and sent to eternal torment] **will be comparable to ten virgins, who took their lamps and went out to meet the bridegroom. Five of them were foolish, and five were prudent."**

Later, after the wise virgins have entered the place of the wedding feast and the door has been shut, the foolish virgins return and ask to be let in, and the bridegroom answers in **verse 12: "Truly I say to you, I do not know you."** In this parable Jesus is the bridegroom (see Chapter 11, "The Marriage of the Lamb"). The wise virgins represent the believing mortals surviving the tribulation, prepared for His return and the subsequent wedding feast, and the foolish virgins are the unprepared unbelievers (apparently professing Christians), who do not enter the kingdom.

Notice that in the parable the wise virgins took oil with them, and the foolish virgins did not. Oil, especially the olive oil commonly used in lamps in Biblical times, is used figuratively in the Bible to represent the Holy Spirit, which of course only the true believers would have. See the previous discussion of the two witnesses in Chapter 6, The First Half of the Tribulation.

Zechariah seems to be referring to this judgment of the children of Israel in **Zechariah 13:8-9:**
    "It will come about in all the land,"
    Declares the LORD,
    "That two parts in it will be cut off *and* perish,
    But the third will be left in it.
    And I will bring the third part through the fire,
    Refine them as silver is refined,
    And test them as gold is tested,
    They will call on My name,
    And I will answer them;
    I will say, 'They are My people,'
    And they will say, 'The LORD is my God.'" (See also Malachi 3:1-5.)

At first glance, this prophecy seems to conflict with **Romans 11:26-27: and so all Israel will be saved; just as it is written,**
    "THE DELIVERER WILL COME FROM ZION,
    HE WILL REMOVE UNGODLINESS FROM JACOB
    THIS IS MY COVENANT WITH THEM,
    WHEN I TAKE AWAY THEIR SINS." [quoting Isaiah 59:20-21]

However, a closer look at both passages, and reconciliation with the passages from Ezekiel and Zechariah quoted above, indicate that the **all Israel** that Paul is talking about are those entering the millennial kingdom after the judgment described by Zechariah 13:8-9 and Ezekiel 20:33-38. Only the believing and therefore saved children of Israel will enter the land of Israel at the beginning of the millennial kingdom.

B. The Basis For Judgment Explained.

In the parable of the talents (Matthew 25:14-30), Jesus explains the basis for His judgment (*i.e.,* how He separates those mortals who are to remain and enter the kingdom from those who are to be removed and condemned to eternal torment). Note that the parable begins in **Matthew 25:14: "For *it*** [*it, i.e.,* the kingdom of heaven, meaning the judgment separating those mortals who will enter the kingdom from those who will not, as noted above] **is just like a man about to go on a journey,...."** In this well-known parable, the master (who represents Jesus) is preparing to leave on a journey, and gives three slaves five, two and one talent, respectively, **"each according to his own ability."** (v.15) Each talent is about 75 pounds of silver, a considerable amount of money.

On his return, the master finds that two have invested the talents entrusted to them wisely and have doubled their talents, while the third slave, who obviously does not like the master, has not even attempted to invest the talent, but has hidden it in the ground. The first two are told **"Well done, good and <u>faithful</u> slave. You were <u>faithful</u> with a few things, I will put you in charge of many things; enter into the joy of your master." Matthew 25:21.** At the end of the parable, after expressing his anger at the third slave, the master says, **"Throw out the worthless slave into the outer darkness; in that place there will be weeping and gnashing of teeth." Matthew 25:30.**

Since the first two slaves enter the kingdom and the third slave is sent to the place of torment (killed), the talents can only represent the faith (to trust in Christ for salvation) given to each person by God. The whole message of the Bible, and especially the New Testament, is that no one is saved by works, but only by faith, and that faith comes from God:

Romans 12:3b: God has allotted to each a measure of faith.

Ephesians 2:8-9: For by grace you have been saved through faith; and that not of yourselves, *it is* the gift of God; not as a result of works, so that no one may boast.

John 3:36 [NIV]**:** [John the Baptist speaking to his disciples] **"Whoever believes in the Son has eternal life, but whoever rejects the Son will not see life, for God's wrath remains on him."** (See also John 3:18)

This parable of the talents is reassuring to all believers, because it confirms what we believe concerning salvation in Jesus' own words, while referring to an end times judgment welcoming believers into the millennial kingdom and condemning unbelievers to physical death followed by spiritual death (eternal separation from God). As Paul wrote in **Romans 1:16: For I am not ashamed of the gospel, for it is the power of God for salvation to everyone who believes, to the Jew first and also to the Greek.**

But there is also a lesson in the master's words scolding the unfaithful slave:

"'You wicked, lazy slave, you knew that I reap where I did not sow and gather where I scattered no seed. [The master is quoting the slave's own wicked assessment of the master in verse 24.] **Then you ought to have put my money in the bank, and on my arrival I would have received my money back with interest. Therefore take away the talent from him, and give it to the one who has the ten talents.'" Matthew 25:26-28.**

Note the anger of the master (representing God's wrath). The implication is clear: the third slave, although given less faith than the first two, was given enough faith to be saved.

If the third slave was given insufficient faith to be saved, there is no reason for a loving God (who suffered humiliation, scourging and a horrible death on a cross to redeem him) to be angry with him. <u>The master can only be angry for the slave's failure to do what he has the power to do</u>. As the master said, all he had to do was apply that faith that was given to him (John 1:12). All the third slave had to do to was take the talent (the faith God had given him) and <u>put it in the bank</u> (v.27).

Since the third slave apparently represents those given the least amount of faith, and the master is angry with him for not applying the talent (faith), a fair conclusion would be that <u>everyone is given enough faith to be saved</u>, but left with ultimate choice of applying or not applying that faith (see John 1:12-13, quoted below), resulting in salvation or condemnation.

Could a loving God do otherwise? Not to give some enough faith to be saved would be to condemn them to eternal torment with no chance of salvation, which does not harmonize with the fact that Christ paid for all sins, not just the sins of believers (John 3:14-17; I Peter 3:18). Neither does it harmonize with the will of God expressed in **1Timothy 2:3-4: This is good and acceptable in the sight of God our Savior, who desires all men to be saved and to come to the knowledge of the truth.** A similar expression of God's will for all to be saved is found in 2 Peter 3:9.

Neither would a loving God create beings "in His own image" as puppets with no choice of where they spend eternity, God making that choice for them. Either option would violate God's character of love and absolute justice. God's sovereignty does not demand that He <u>causes</u> all things to happen (*e.g.*, that He created evil).

He is, after all, omnipotent and accountable only to His own immutable characteristics, which include love and absolute justice. There is nothing in His character to prevent Him from giving all His sentient created beings the ability to choose to accept or reject His grace and the opportunity to spend eternity with Him. The Scriptures, taken as a whole, tell us that is exactly what He did, first with the angels and then with mankind.

<u>C. The Judgment of the Nations (Gentiles)</u>.

Jesus next describes the judgment of the remaining mortals, the Gentiles, in Matthew 25:31-46. He first sets the stage in **Matthew 25:31-33** [NIV]: **"When the Son of Man comes in his glory, and all the angels with him, then He will sit on his throne in heavenly glory. All the nations** [*i.e.,* all living Gentile mortals] **will be gathered before him, and he will separate <u>the people</u>** [*not* the nations as whole nations] **one from another, as a shepherd separates the sheep from the goats. He will put the sheep on his right, and the goats on his left."**

He then pronounces judgment in **Matthew 25:34 and 41: [34] "Then the King will say to those on His right, 'Come, you who are blessed of My Father, inherit the kingdom prepared for you from the foundation of the world....'" [41] "Then He will also say to those on His left, 'Depart from Me, accursed ones, into the eternal fire which has been prepared for the devil and his angels....'"** All unbelievers surviving the tribulation are killed, to be resurrected at the great white throne judgment, discussed in Chapter 15.

Jesus also talked of His judgment of mortals at His return in Matthew 13, with the parable of the wheat and the tares (Matthew 13:24-30, 37-43-- **v. 24b: "The kingdom of heaven may be compared to...."**), and the parable of the dragnet (Matthew 13:47-50--**v. 47: "Again, the kingdom of heaven is like a dragnet...."**), both discussed at the start of this Section 5 above.

So what mortals are left to enter the kingdom? Only those made righteous by God's Son on the cross. **But as many as received Him, to them He gave the right to become children of God,** *even* **to those who believe in His name, who were born, not of blood nor of the will of the flesh nor of the will of man, but of God. John 1:12-13.** Jesus makes that clear in His Olivet Discourse (Matthew 24-25), and from the parables in Matthew 13. He also makes clear in **Matthew 10:22,28,32-33** that it is **"the one who has endured to the end who will be saved."** Those who have survived the last half of the tribulation while retaining their faith in Christ's salvation and refusing to receive the mark of the beast or worship his image will certainly have **"endured to the end"**.

So what kind of world will these believing mortals and immortals see in the millennial kingdom? That is the subject of Chapter 13.

<u>6. THE BIG PICTURE</u>

Christ's return to rule (often referred to as the Second Coming), described in Revelation 19:11-16, is followed by the battle of Armageddon in Revelation 19:17-21. After the battle, the beast (antichrist) and the false prophet are thrown into the lake of fire, and Satan and his fallen angels (demons) are imprisoned in the abyss (bottomless pit) for the one-thousand year millennium in which Christ rules on earth.

Israel is regathered, and all mortals who survived the tribulation and the battle of Armageddon, both Jew and Gentile, are judged by Christ, resulting in all unbelievers being killed, leaving only believing mortals to enter the millennial kingdom, with the believing Jews entering the land of Israel. All other believers from every age, both Jew and Gentile, will also be on earth in their resurrected, immortal bodies to celebrate at the marriage supper of the Lamb and rule with (under) Christ in the millennial kingdom, as we will see in the next chapter.

FOR REVIEW: (Cite verses for your answers.)

1. How does the tribulation end? _____

2. Jesus never said He would return to earth. True False _____

3. Jesus' return will be anticipated by Satan and the antichrist. True False _____

4. Where and when does the battle of Armageddon take place? _____
_____

5. What happens to the antichrist and the false prophet after the battle of Armageddon?
_____

6. What happens to Satan and his fallen angels after the battle of Armageddon?
_____

7. Why aren't Satan and his fallen angels killed after the battle of Armageddon?
_____

8. What people are gathered from all over the world at Christ's return? _____

9. Where are they taken? _____

10. What happens to them there? _____

11. Who among them enters the land of Israel? _____

12. Who are the "elect" of Matthew 24:31? _____

13. Will the Old Testament Jewish saints be resurrected? _____

14. Are the Old Testament Gentile saints and the martyred tribulation saints resurrected?
_____

15. In Matthew 24:40 and 41, Jesus talks of one being taken, and one being left. Who is taken and who is left?
_____

16. What does the oil represent in the parable of the ten virgins? _____

17. What do the talents represent in the parable of the talents? _____

18. What did the third slave do with the talent given to him? _____

19. What happened to the third slave in the parable of the talents and to the goats in the judgment of the nations? _____

20. What mortals are left alive to enter the millennium? _____

21. What immortals in glorified bodies enter the millennium? _____
_____

22. Are there any Old Testament references to the battle of Armageddon? _____
_____

CHAPTER THIRTEEN
THE MILLENNIAL KINGDOM

MAIN IDEA: Christ rules on a beautifully restored earth for 1000 years of peace, prosperity, good health and long life for mortals. It is a time of absolute justice, great joy and harmony, with special blessings for, and fulfillment of all God's Old Testament promises to, the nation of Israel.

The focal point of **the day of the LORD** is Christ's rule on earth during what He often called **the kingdom of heaven** (*e.g.,* Matthew 13:24,44; 18:3,4; 19:14; 20:1; 25:1) and **the kingdom of God** (*e.g.,* John 3:3, Luke 22:16, 18). This kingdom age begins with all saints from every age, either in their resurrected, immortal bodies, or as mortal believers who survived the tribulation period dwelling on a restored earth under Christ's rule.

The world is radically transformed during this time. The many changes are discussed in the following sections:

1. CHRIST RULES ON EARTH
A. Christ's kingdom on the present earth will last one thousand years.
B. Christ rules the entire earth.

2. THE IMMORTAL SAINTS RULE WITH CHRIST
A. David is king (prince under Christ's rule) over Israel
B. The twelve apostles rule the twelve tribes of Israel
C. Resurrected saints rule with Christ.

3. MORTALS LIVING IN THE KINGDOM
A. Mortals are ruled by Christ with absolute justice.
B. Mortals lead long, healthy lives.
C. Mortals enjoy worldwide peace.
D. Mortals enjoy a restored earth.
E. Mortals will not be influenced by Satan and his fallen angels.

4. ISRAEL IS THE CENTER OF THE WORLD
A. The covenant with Abram is fulfilled.
B. The land of Israel is transformed.
C. Jerusalem is the center of world-wide rule and worship.
D. The kingdom is a time of great joy in Israel.
E. The wealth of the world flows into Israel.
F. Israel dwells in security.

5. OVERVIEW OF THE MILLENIAL KINGDOM

The Old Testament prophets knew that YHWH (see Exodus 6:2-3), often translated "the LORD," would rule during this future time of great promise for Israel:

Isaiah 2:2-4:
>**Now it will come about that
>In the last days
>The mountain of the house of the LORD
>Will be established as the chief of the mountains,
>And will be raised above the hills;
>And all the nations will stream to it.
>And many peoples will come and say,
>"Come, let us go up to the mountain of the LORD,
>To the house of the God of Jacob;
>That He may teach us concerning His ways
>And that we may walk in His paths."
>For the law will go forth from Zion
>And the word of the LORD from Jerusalem.
>And He will judge between the nations,
>And will render decisions for many peoples;
>And they will hammer their swords into plowshares and their spears
>   into pruning hooks.
>Nation will not lift up sword against nation,
>And never again will they learn war.** (See Micah 4:1-3.)

Ezekiel saw the LORD ruling from the millennial temple on top of **the mountain of the house of the LORD** (see above) in a vision described in Ezekiel 40-44. **Ezekiel 43: 4-7a: And the glory of the LORD came into the house** [temple] **by the way of the gate facing toward the east. And the Spirit lifted me up and brought me into the inner court; and behold, the glory of the LORD filled the house. Then I heard one speaking to me from the house, while a man was standing beside me. He said to me, "Son of man,** *this is* **the place of My throne and the place of the soles of My feet, where I will dwell among the sons of Israel forever."**

1. CHRIST RULES ON EARTH

[**T**]**he LORD** in these and many other Old Testament prophecies is Christ Himself: **Matthew 19:28: And Jesus said to them** [His disciples], **"Truly I say to you, that you who have followed Me, in the regeneration** [of the earth during the millennial kingdom] **when the Son of Man will sit on His glorious throne, you also shall sit upon twelve thrones, judging the twelve tribes of Israel."**

Those around Jesus understood that He was going to rule in the predicted kingdom. **Matthew 20:20-21: Then the mother of the sons of Zebedee came to Jesus with her sons, bowing down and making a request of Him. And He said to her, "What do you wish?" She said to Him, "Command that <u>in Your kingdom</u> these two sons of mine may sit one on Your right and one on Your** left."

The thief on the cross knew that Christ was going to rule in His kingdom: **Luke 23:42: And he was saying, "Jesus, remember me when You come in Your kingdom!"**

How long will the kingdom last? Over whom will He rule? What will the earth be like during this time? What will life be like for those mortals living then? What will be the role of Israel and Jerusalem during His rule? What influence will Satan and his angels have? Will we, the saints (believers) now alive, be there? We will examine the answers to these questions in this chapter.

A. *Christ's kingdom on the present earth will last one thousand years.*

Revelation 20:6 Blessed and holy is the one who has a part in the first resurrection; over these the second death has no power, but they will be priests of God and of Christ and will reign with Him <u>for a thousand years.</u>

Revelation 20:2, 3, 4 and 7 also mentions a thousand years as the duration of the kingdom. It is from this reference that Christians and Bible scholars refer to this time as "the millennium." Old Testament writers and Jesus referred to it as **the kingdom of heaven** or **the kingdom of God** (*See e.g.* John 3:3). It is therefore called the millennial kingdom here, to avoid confusion.

Revelation 20 contains the <u>only</u> reference to the duration of the kingdom age. Old Testament prophets had no idea how long the kingdom age would last, and often confused it with the future eternity in the new Jerusalem, the subject Chapter 16.

B. *Christ rules the entire earth.*

The millennial kingdom is headquartered in Jerusalem, with Christ's throne in the temple there. (See Ezekiel 4-7a quoted above.) Although His attention is focused on Israel as God once more turns His attention to His chosen people, Christ's rule extends over the entire earth:

Daniel 7:13-14a:
    I kept looking in the night visions,
    And behold, with the clouds of heaven
    One like a <u>Son of Man</u> was coming [See Matthew 24:30.]
    And He came up to the Ancient of Days
    And was presented before Him.
    And to Him was given dominion,
    Glory and <u>a kingdom,</u>
    <u>That all the peoples, nations and *men of every* language</u>
    <u>Might serve Him.</u>

In **Isaiah 2:4a**, quoted at the beginning of this chapter, we also see that during this time **He will judge between the nations**, indicating world-wide rule.

2. THE IMMORTAL SAINTS RULE WITH CHRIST

A. David is king (prince under Christ's rule) over Israel.

Several of the Old Testament prophets tell us David, obviously in his immortal, resurrected body, will rule over Israel during this time:

Hosea 3:4-5:
For the sons of Israel will remain for many days without king or prince, without sacrifice or *sacred* **pillar and without ephod or household idols. Afterward the sons of Israel will return and seek the L**ORD **their God and David their king; and they will come trembling to the L**ORD **and to His goodness in the last days.**

Ezekiel 37: 24-25: [The word of the LORD, v.15]
"My servant David will be king over them, and they will all have one shepherd; and they will walk in My ordinances and keep My statutes and observe them. They shall live on the land that I gave to Jacob My servant, in which your fathers lived; and they will live on it, they and their sons and their sons' sons, forever; and David My servant shall be their prince forever...."

Jeremiah 30:9: ["Thus says the LORD,...." v.2]
'But they shall serve the LORD **their God and David their king, whom I will raise up for them.'..."**

B. The twelve apostles rule the twelve tribes of Israel.

Matthew 19:28: and Jesus said to them [the apostles], **"Truly I say to you, that you who have followed Me, in the regeneration when the Son of Man will sit on His glorious throne, you also shall sit upon twelve thrones, judging the twelve tribes of Israel...."**

C. Resurrected saints rule with Christ.

Revelation 20:6: Blessed and holy is the one who has a part in the first resurrection; over these the second death has no power, but they will be priests of God and of Christ and will reign with Him for a thousand years.

Daniel 7:27: [one of those who were standing by **in Daniel's vision (v.16), a heavenly being, probably an angel, is the one speaking to Daniel**] ["]**'Then the sovereignty, the dominion and the greatness of all the kingdoms under the whole heaven will be given to the people of the saints of the Highest One...'**["].

Revelation 5:9-10: And they [heavenly beings, v.8] **sang a new song, saying,**

"Worthy are You to take the book and to break the seals; for You were slain, and purchased for God with Your blood *men* **from every tribe and tongue and people and nation.**

"You have made them [those purchased] *to be* **a kingdom and priests to our God; and <u>they will reign upon the earth</u>."**

Note that the resurrected, immortal saints will rule <u>upon the earth</u>. The question then becomes, do they leave their home in the new Jerusalem (discussed in a later chapter), the place Jesus has prepared for them (John 14:2-3), to live on the restored earth (the home of the Bridegroom) during this one thousand years? Scripture doesn't seem clear on where the saints reside during this time. However, if the pattern of the traditional Jewish wedding is followed, then Christ's bride, the church, will dwell with Him on the earth during the 1000 years.

For those wondering, Scripture does not tell us when mortal believers who die during the millennial kingdom will receive their immortal glorified bodies, and whether they will rule as immortals during this time.

<u>3. MORTALS LIVING IN THE KINGDOM</u>

We saw in the judgments that took place prior to the start of the millennial kingdom (See Chapter 12, "Christ Returns to Rule.") that only mortals who are believers are left alive on earth to enter the kingdom. Jesus summed it up for Nicodemus this way in **John 3:3: "Truly, truly, I say to you, unless one is born again he cannot see the kingdom of God."** However, their life experiences will be significantly different from ours.

Their world will be as close to perfect as God can make it in a world where people (1) are mortal and (2) are still given the right to choose whether to accept or reject God and His plan of salvation and whether to choose to follow God's will or their own decisions in the way they live.

A. *<u>Mortals are ruled by Christ with absolute justice.</u>*

One of the attributes of God is absolute justice, which will be a significant part of Christ's rule. Note that Christ will **judge between the nations** during this time (See **Isaiah 2:4a**, quoted above), indicating that conflicts arise, a sign that <u>mortal men have significant (if not ruling) authority over the decisions of at least some nations in the millennial kingdom</u>.

If Christ is resolving conflicts between the nations, apparently someone in authority is not following the will of God. All the glimpses Scripture gives us of the immortals living in the presence of God, in both the Old and New Testaments, show all immortals, both angels and resurrected saints (*see e.g., Revelation 7:9-12*), following the will of God. **Revelation 22:3a: There will no longer be any**

curse.... The curse is spiritual death, the result of sin.

The immortal saints have passed from death into life (1 John 3:14), and can no longer sin, *i.e.,* do something contrary to the will of God. They are forever "in tune" with the will of God. We can look forward to that freedom from sin in eternity. *"While God's will is our law, we are but a kind of noble slaves; when [H]is will is our will, we are free children [of God]."*--George MacDonald, *David Elginbrod*. How blessed we will be in eternity to have the freedom that comes with no longer being able to think or do anything contrary to the will of God!

In contrast, mortal men, even believers no longer "slaves to sin", still have their fleshly desire to sin, *i.e.,* to do something contrary to the will of God. Paul described his internal war against this fleshly desire in Romans 7:15-25.

If neither the angels nor the immortal saints in glorified bodies can do anything contrary to the will of God, only <u>mortals</u> present in the millennial kingdom have that ability. (Remember, the only immortals who still have that ability are bound in the abyss (bottomless pit) during this one thousand years.) If Christ has to judge between the nations, as indicated by Isaiah 2:4a, a <u>mortal</u> in authority is not following His will, and is ultimately subject to Christ's judgment during this time.

Concerning His judgment of disputes between individuals (mortals) Isaiah says:

Isaiah 11:3-4:
>**And He will delight in the fear of the LORD,**
>**And He will not judge by what His eyes see,**
>**Nor make a decision by what His ears hear;**
>**But with righteousness He will judge the poor,**
>**And decide with fairness for the afflicted of the earth;**
>**And He will strike the earth with the rod of His mouth,**
>**And with the breath of His lips He will slay the wicked.**

He will be judging on the basis of (His) righteousness. Christ is both judge and executioner, and there does not appear a lot of time between the sentencing and punishment phase of the trial. Neither will the oppressed have to wait years for justice to be done:

Isaiah 65:24: [the LORD speaking] **"It will also come to pass that before they call, I will answer; and while they are still speaking, I will hear."**

In this passage, the LORD may be referring to a cry for help or mercy, but a cry for justice also seems to be indicated, implying instant justice.

Isaiah 29:20:
>**For the ruthless will come to an end and the scorner will be finished.**
>**Indeed all who are intent on doing evil will be cut off.....**

Absolute justice, indeed. For those victimized by wrongdoing, a blessing. For the rebellious and the evildoers, not so much.

B. *Mortals lead long, healthy lives.*

Isaiah 65:20-22: [the Lord GOD speaking, v. 13]
> "**No longer will there be in it** [the earth during the millennial kingdom] **an infant who lives but a few days,**
> **Or an old man who does not live out his days;**
> **For the youth will die at the age of one hundred**
> **And the one who does not reach the age of one hundred**
> **Shall be thought accursed.**
> **They shall build houses and inhabit them;**
> **They shall also plant vineyards and eat their fruit.**
> **They shall not build and another inhabit,**
> **They shall not plant and another eat;**
> **For as the lifetime of a tree, so shall be the days of My people,**
> **And My chosen ones shall wear out the work of their hands.**"

Isaiah 29:18:
> **On that day the deaf shall hear words of a book,**
> **And out of *their* gloom and darkness the eyes of the blind shall see.**

Isaiah 33:24a:
> **And no resident will say, "I am sick"....**

Isaiah 35:5-6a:
> **Then the eyes of the blind will be opened**
> **And the ears of the deaf will be unstopped.**
> **Then the lame will leap like a deer,**
> **And the tongue of the mute will shout for joy.**

Jesus quoted the Isaiah 35:5-6a passage in Matthew 11:5, to assure John the Baptist that He was indeed the Messiah who would one day bring in the kingdom. However, the ultimate fulfillment of the passage appears to be in the millennial kingdom, where the healing will be widespread, probably worldwide.

C. *Mortals enjoy worldwide peace.*

The beautiful passage from Isaiah 2:2-4 quoted at the beginning of the chapter ends with the line: **And never again will they learn war. Isaiah 2:4b.** The entire passage shows the millennial kingdom as a time of peace, with Christ ruling and settling all disagreements between the nations, making war pointless, not that He would permit it during this time in any event.

D. *Mortals enjoy a restored earth.*

All of creation is now corrupted by mankind's sin, beginning with Adam:

Romans 8:20-22: For the creation was subjected to futility, not willingly, but because of Him who subjected it, in hope that the creation itself also will be set free from its slavery to corruption into the freedom of the glory of the children of God. For we know that the whole creation groans and suffers the pains of childbirth together until now.

The corruption of creation <u>ends</u> with the start of the millennial kingdom when the earth is restored, and the result is a beautiful picture of peace and joy:

Isaiah 55: 12:
> **For you will go out with joy**
> **And be led forth with peace;**
> **The mountains and the hills will break forth into shouts of joy before you,**
> **And all the trees of the field will clap *their* hands,**
> **Instead of the thorn bush the cypress will come up,**
> **And instead of the nettle the myrtle will come up....**

Isaiah 11:6-9:

> **And the wolf will dwell with the lamb,**
> **And the leopard will lie down with the young goat,**
> **And the calf and the young lion and the fatling together;**
> **And a little boy will lead them.**
> **Also the cow and the bear will graze,**
> **Their young will lie down together,**
> **And the lion will eat straw like the ox.**
> **The nursing child will play by the hole of the cobra,**
> **And the weaned child will put his hand on the viper's den.**
> **They will not hurt or destroy in all My holy mountain,**
> **For the earth will be full of the knowledge of the Lord**
> **As the waters cover the sea.**

In Israel itself, the landscape is radically changed, as we will see when we examine God's blessings on His chosen people, below.

E. *Mortals will not be influenced by Satan and his fallen angels.*

As we saw in the previous chapter, at the conclusion of the battle of Armageddon, Satan and his fallen angels will be removed from the earthly realm and thrown into what various translations call **the abyss**, **the pit** or **the bottomless pit**, and imprisoned for the entire 1000 years of the millennial kingdom:

Revelation 20:1-4: Then I saw an angel coming down from heaven, holding the key of the abyss and a great chain in his hand. And he laid hold of the dragon, the serpent of old, who is the devil and Satan, and bound him for a thousand years; and he threw him into the abyss, and shut *it* **and sealed** *it* **over him, so that he would not deceive the nations any longer, until the thousand years were completed; after these things he must be released for a short time.**

So Satan definitely will not be present. As for his fallen angels, Isaiah tells us:

Isaiah 24:21-22:
So it will happen in that day,
That the LORD **will punish <u>the host of heaven on high</u>,**
And the kings of the earth on earth.
They will be gathered together
Like **prisoners in the dungeon,**
And <u>will be confined in prison</u>;
And after many days they will be punished.

The **hosts of heaven on high** can only refer to the fallen angels who followed Satan in his rebellion against God, described in Isaiah 14:12-14 and Ezekiel 28:12b-19. They apparently are the angels described in **Revelation 12:4: And his** (Satan's) **tail swept away a third of the stars of heaven and threw them to the earth.** Consequently, these verses tell us that <u>all Satanic and demonic influence will be removed from earth during the 1000 years.</u> No one will be able to truthfully say, "The devil made me do it."

We shall see in the next chapter, however, that even without that evil influence, even in the perfect conditions created during this time, the heart of man can still rebel against God, and when these evil influences reappear on earth, men are easily persuaded to openly rebel against God.

<u>4. ISRAEL IS THE CENTER OF THE WORLD</u>

The millennial kingdom is centered in Jerusalem and on Israel and its people in every way. We have seen that Christ centers His world government in Jerusalem. Worship and economic prosperity are also concentrated in Jerusalem and Israel. This is the time God has promised to the people of Israel, frequently described by the Old Testament prophets, a promise all the way back to Abram, through Isaac and Jacob, to be fulfilled <u>after</u> **the fullness of the Gentiles has come in**.

Romans 11:25-27: For I do not want you brethren, to be uninformed of this mystery--so that you will not be wise in your own estimation--that a partial hardening has happened to Israel until the fullness of the Gentiles has come in; and so all Israel will be saved; just as it is written,

"THE DELIVERER WILL COME FROM ZION;
HE WILL REMOVE UNGODLINESS FROM JACOB
THIS IS MY COVENANT WITH THEM,
WHEN I TAKE AWAY THEIR SINS."

The **fullness of the Gentiles** appears to come in when Jesus returns at the battle of Armageddon to judge and then to rule in His kingdom, as discussed in the previous chapter, "Christ Returns to Rule." God's focus then returns to Israel, which enjoys special blessings during these one thousand years.

A. *The covenant to Abram is fulfilled.*

The kingdom described by the Old Testament prophets is first and foremost a restoration of the greatness of the ancient kingdom of Israel, apparently expanded to include all the area promised to Abram in **Genesis 15:18:**
On that day the LORD made a covenant with Abram, saying,
  "To your descendants I have given this land,
  From the river of Egypt [the Nile] **as far as the great river, the river**
    Euphrates: ..."

We see Israel's boundaries extended:
Isaiah 26: 15:
  You have increased the nation, O LORD
  You have increased the nation, You are glorified;
  You have extended all the borders of the land.

Most of the land will be divided among the twelve tribes of Israel, with certain portions set aside for the city (Jerusalem), the priests (*i.e.,* the sons of Zadok who remained faithful), called the holy allotment, and the prince (David), all as described in Ezekiel 47:13-21, and Ezekiel 48. However, areas north of Damascus and south of the **brook *of* Egypt** [v.28] will not be given to the tribes for residential purposes, although there is no reason to suppose that the covenant with Abram is not fulfilled, which leaves these areas to the north and south part of Israel in the millennial kingdom, but not designated for a special use.

B. *The land of Israel is transformed.*

Ezekiel 36:33: [the LORD speaking] '**Thus says the Lord GOD, "On the day that I cleanse you from all your iniquities, I will cause the cities to be inhabited, and the waste places will be rebuilt. The desolate land will be cultivated instead of being a desolation in the sight of everyone who passes by. <u>They will say, 'This desolate land has become like the garden of Eden</u>; and the waste, desolate and ruined cities are fortified and inhabited.'... "**

In Israel itself, the landscape is radically changed into a lush paradise. Mt. Zion (Jerusalem) is raised up to be **the chief of the mountains** as Isaiah tells us in Isaiah 2:2 (quoted at the beginning of the chapter), and streams flow throughout the land:

Ezekiel 40:2: In the visions of God He brought me into the land of Israel and set me on a <u>very high mountain</u>, and on it to the south there was a structure like a city. [Jerusalem]

Zechariah 14:10: All the land will be changed into a plain from Geba to Rimmon south of Jerusalem; but Jerusalem will rise and remain on its site ....

Isaiah 35:6b-8a:
> **For waters will break forth in the wilderness**
> **And streams in the Arabah** [desert]
> **The scorched land will become a pool**
> **And the thirsty ground springs of water;**
> **In the haunts of jackals, its resting place**
> **Grass *becomes* reeds and rushes.**
> **A highway will be there, a roadway,**
> **And it will be called the Highway of Holiness.**

Ezekiel 47 begins with a description of a river flowing from under the east gate of the millennial temple down to the dead sea, making it fresh, then says in **Ezekiel 47:9:** [the man (the LORD?) of Ezekiel 40:2 is speaking] **"It will come about that every living creature which swarms in every place where the river goes, will live. And there will be very many fish, for these waters go there and the others become fresh; so everything will live where the river goes."**

Zechariah 14:8: And it will come about in that day that living waters will flow out of Jerusalem, half of them toward the eastern sea and the other half toward the western sea; it will be in summer as well as in winter.

Isaiah 27:6:
> **In the days to come Jacob will take root,**
> **Israel will blossom and sprout,**
> **And they will fill the whole world with fruit.**

C. *Jerusalem is the center of world-wide rule and worship.*

Ezekiel chapters 40-46 describe in great detail the millennial temple in Jerusalem and the sacrificial ceremonies that will take place during this time. Earlier in this chapter we reviewed Ezekiel 43:4:7a, which tells us that Christ will physically dwell in the temple and His throne (from which He will rule the world) will be in the temple during His reign in the millennial kingdom. We see in Isaiah that this center of worship will not just be for Israel:

Isaiah 2:2-3:
>Now it will come about that
>In the last days
>The mountain of the house of the LORD
>Will be established as the chief of the mountains,
>And will be raised above the hills;
>And <u>all the nations will stream to it.</u>
>And <u>many peoples</u> will come and say,
>"Come, let us go up to the mountain of the LORD,
>To the house of the God of Jacob;
>That He may teach us concerning His ways
>And that we may walk in His paths."

D. *The kingdom is a time of great joy in Israel.*

Isaiah 35:10:
>And the ransomed of the LORD will return
>And come with joyful shouting to Zion,
>With everlasting joy upon their heads.
>They will find gladness and joy,
>And sorrow and sighing will flee away.

Zephaniah 3:14-17: [the LORD speaking, v.8]
>Shout for joy, O daughter of Zion!
>"Shout in *triumph*, O Israel!
>Rejoice and exult with all *your* heart,
>O daughter of Jerusalem!
>The LORD has taken away *His* judgments against you,
>He has cleared away your enemies.
>The King of Israel, the LORD, is in your midst;
>You will fear disaster no more.
>In that day it will be said to Jerusalem:
>Do not be afraid, O Zion;
>Do not let your hands fall limp.
>The LORD your God is in your midst,
>A victorious warrior.
>He will exult over you with joy.
>He will be quiet in His love.
>He will rejoice over you with shouts of joy...."

See also Isaiah 55:12, quoted in section 3D above.

E. *The wealth of the world flows into Israel.*

Many passages describe Israel's wealth during this time of God's fulfillment of His promises to His chosen people. All of chapter 60 and much of chapter 61 of Isaiah talk of Israel's prosperity during this time. We have space to examine only parts of these chapters.

Isaiah 60:5: [the LORD speaking]
> "Then you [Israel] **will see and be radiant,**
> **And your heart will thrill and rejoice;**
> **Because the abundance of the sea** [Gentile nations] **will be turned to**
>   **you,**
> <u>**The wealth of the nations will come to you.**</u>"

Isaiah 60:11-12: [the LORD speaking]
> "**Your gates will be open continually;**
> **They will not be closed day or night,**
> <u>**So that *men* may bring to you the wealth of the nations,**</u>
> **With their kings led in procession.**
> **For the nation and the kingdom which will not serve you will perish,**
> **And the nations will be utterly ruined. ...**"

Isaiah 61:6:
> **But you** [Israel] **will be called the priests of the LORD;**
> **You will be spoken of *as* ministers of our God.**
> <u>**You will eat the wealth of nations,**</u>
> **And in their riches you will boast.**

F. Israel dwells in security.

For the first time since the reign of Solomon, Israel will be secure in the land, enjoying the blessings of the millennial kingdom:

Zechariah 14:11: People will live in it [Jerusalem]**, and there will be no more curse, for Jerusalem will dwell in security.**

Ezekiel 34:25, 28: [Lord GOD speaking, v.11]
"**I will make a covenant of peace with them and eliminate harmful beasts from the land so that they may live securely in the wilderness and sleep in the woods.... They will no longer be a prey to the nations, and the beasts of the earth will not devour them; but will live securely, and no one will make *them* afraid.**"

Jeremiah 23:6a: [the LORD speaking, v.1]
> "**In His days Judah will be saved,**
> **And Israel will dwell securely;...**"

Those who doubt God's faithfulness to Israel and His determination to make His chosen people a special nation, elevated among all others, would do well to heed the words of the LORD in **Isaiah 49:15:**
> "**Can a woman forget her nursing child**
> **And have no compassion on the son of her womb?**
> **Even these may forget; but I will not forget you** [Israel]**. ...**"

God's central purpose in everything He does in the millennial kingdom is to fulfill His promised blessings to the nation of Israel. We Gentile believers are blessed "to be along for the ride." We will literally see the closest thing possible to "heaven on (this) earth."

5. OVERVIEW OF THE MILLENIAL KINGDOM

At Christ's return (the "second coming"), He regathers the nation of Israel, removes (kills) all unbelievers, and places all the Jewish believers in a beautifully restored nation of Israel. Christ and the immortal saints (believers) who lived as mortals from the time of Adam to the time they died during the tribulation period rule on the restored earth for one thousand years.

Mortals living during this time will live long, healthy lives. There will be one thousand years of peace, health, prosperity and justice. Although only believing mortals enter the kingdom, many mortals are born during this time, and not all are believers, setting the stage for the battle of Gog and Magog, the subject of our next chapter.

FOR REVIEW: (Cite verses for your answers.)

1. Who rules the world during the millennial kingdom? _____

2. Why is this time called "the millennium" by Bible scholars? _____

3. Where is Christ during this 1000 years? _____

4. Describe Jerusalem during this 1000 years. _____
_____

5. What other cities are mentioned in the prophecies of the millennium? _____

6. Describe the physical changes in the land of Israel during this time. _____
_____

7. How will the lives of mortals living in the millennium be different from our lives today?
_____
_____

8. What happens to the nation of Israel during the millennium? _____
_____

CHAPTER FOURTEEN
THE FINAL BATTLE

MAIN IDEA: At the end of the millennium, after one thousand years of Christ's perfect rule in a beautifully restored earth, Satan and his fallen angels are released and quickly gather a huge army of rebellious mortals to attack Jerusalem. Fire comes down from heaven and kills the mortal army. Satan and his angels are thrown into the lake of fire.

Revelation 20:7-10: When the thousand years are completed, Satan will be released from his prison, and will come out to deceive the nations which are in the four corners of the earth, Gog and Magog, to gather them together for the war; the number of them is like the sand of the seashore. And they came up on the broad plain of the earth and surrounded the camp of the saints and the beloved city, and fire came down from heaven and devoured them. And the devil who deceived them was thrown into the lake of fire and brimstone, where the beast and the false prophet are also; and they will be tormented day and night forever and ever.

After one thousand years of Christ's world-wide perfect rule on a restored earth, without the presence of Satan and his fallen angels, Satan (and probably his angels) are released, and have no trouble gathering a huge army of men to attack Jerusalem and the throne of Christ Himself. After all the blessings bestowed upon mortals in the millennial kingdom and after living with Christ in their presence, administering perfect government and perfect justice for one thousand years, when Satan comes calling, men still choose to rebel against God.

This not only says something about the men rebelling, it should also remind us of who we really are in and of ourselves. Let us not forget to be thankful to God for making us **a new creature** in Christ (**2 Corinthians 5:17**), nor forget how easily we can fall back into our fleshly rebellion if we take our eyes off our Savior. Peter's walk on the water described in Matthew 14:25-32 comes to mind. As soon as he was distracted by the wind, his faith in Jesus wavered, and he began to sink. Are we any different?

Jeremiah 17:9: The heart [of man] ***is* deceitful above all *things*, and desperately wicked: who can know it?** [KJV]

<u>1. A comparison of Armageddon and the battle of Gog and Magog.</u>

Before looking at the details of this final battle, it is worth taking a moment to compare the two end times battles, the battle Armageddon and the battle of Gog and Magog. Both battles start out looking like a stage set for a giant battle, but turn out to be very one-sided slaughters. This should not be a surprise when on one side of the battle is the Almighty God-Creator Himself. There are, however, several significant differences between the two battles that should be noted:

First, a brief comparison of the two battles:

THE BATTLE OF ARMAGEDDON	THE BATTLE OF GOG AND MAGOG
A. *Timing.* Armageddon occurs at Christ's return, <u>before</u> the 1000 year reign of Christ.	A. *Timing.* The battle takes place <u>after</u> the 1000 year reign of Christ.
B. *Location.* Near the Mount of Megiddo, in northeast Israel.	B. *Location.* Outside Jerusalem, when the invading army surrounds the city.
C. *Purpose.* The beast assembles the army to make war against Jesus, who is returning to rule on earth.	C. *Purpose.* To plunder Israel, and capture spoil.
D. *Destruction.* The army is destroyed by the sword which comes from the mouth of Jesus.	D. *Destruction.* Fire comes down from heaven and devours them.
E. *Result for Satan.* Satan and his fallen angels are bound in the abyss for 1000 years.	E. *Result for Satan.* Satan and his fallen angels are thrown into the lake of fire, to be tormented there forever.
F. *Result for Unbelievers.* After the battle, all unbelievers are judged by Christ and removed (killed).	F. *Result for Unbelievers.* We are not told, but the next significant event is the destruction of the universe by fire.

Now for a look at the Scriptural references:

A. *The battles take place 1000 years apart.*

The battle of Armageddon takes place before the start of the millennial kingdom, when Christ returns to earth (Rev. 19:11-21)

The battle of Gog and Magog takes place at its end, one thousand years later. (Rev. 20:7-10; Ezekiel 38-39, describing Israel as it will only exist at the end of the millennium, as discussed in detail below)

B. *The battles occur (i.e., the invading armies gather) in different parts of Israel.*

The battle of Armageddon apparently occurs in the valley near the Mount of Megiddo, variously called Armageddon, the plain of Esdraelon and the Valley of Megiddo (Revelation 16:16), where Satan and his minions have gathered together armies from **the kings of the whole world** (**Revelation 16:14**) to battle the returning King, Jesus, and his heavenly armies. This valley is located in northeast Israel, away from Jerusalem.

In the final battle of Gog and Magog, Gog's army will be **like a cloud covering the land (Ezekiel 38:9,16)**. John tells us the army **surrounded...the beloved city** [Jerusalem] (**Revelation 20:9**). The invading army apparently invades a large part of Israel's land area, not just one valley, and the attack appears to be ultimately focused on Jerusalem, which has been the world's political, spiritual and economic center for the last 1000 years.

C. *The armies gather for different purposes.*

Revelation 16:13-14: And I saw *coming* **out of the mouth of the dragon and out of the mouth of the beast and out of the mouth of the false prophet, three unclean spirits like frogs; for they are spirits of demons, performing signs, which go out to the kings of the whole world, to gather them together <u>for the war of the great day of God, the Almighty.</u>** This army for the battle of Armageddon is gathered by the unholy trinity to fight Christ at His return to rule.

Ezekiel 38:10-12a: 'Thus says the Lord GOD, "It will come about on that day, that thoughts will come into your [Gog's] **mind and you will devise an evil plan, and you will say, 'I will go up against the land of unwalled villages, I will go against those who are at rest, that live securely, all of them living without walls and having no bars or gates, <u>to capture spoil and to seize plunder,</u>** .... The object in this final battle is to plunder the riches of Israel which it has acquired during its time of blessing in the millennial kingdom.

D. *The two armies are destroyed by God in a different manner.*

The armies gathered at Armageddon are **killed with the sword which came from the mouth of Him who sat on the horse…. Revelation 19:21.** Jesus spoke, and they were killed. This should not be a surprise. The spoken word of Jesus was powerful enough to create (*i.e.,* make out of <u>nothing</u>) the entire universe. We are told in **Colossians 1:16: For by Him** [Jesus] **all things were created, both in the heavens and on earth, visible and invisible, whether thrones or dominions or rulers or authorities--all things have been created through Him and for Him.** Similar language appears in John 1:3. These verses seem to say that the Trinity acted in concert at the creation, but that the second member of the Trinity, Who became the incarnate Jesus, was the one who actually spoke the universe into existence in Genesis chapter 1. See also Hebrews 4:12 and Revelation 2:16.

At the battle of Gog and Magog, the invading army, according to the abbreviated account in Revelation 20:9, is killed by fire coming down from heaven, amplified in Ezekiel 38:20-22 to include a great earthquake, internal warfare within the invading army, pestilence, and rain containing hailstones, fire and brimstone.

E. *Satan and his armies are defeated in both battles, but with different results for Satan and his angels.*

The initial results of the two battles are similar. Satan and his angels are defeated. The mortals are killed, but of course all angels, including Satan, are immortal and cannot be killed. After the first battle (Armageddon) they are imprisoned, as we saw in the chapter entitled "Christ Returns to Rule".

After the second battle (Gog and Magog), Satan and his angels are thrown into the lake of fire. We are told Satan is thrown into the lake of fire in Revelation 20:10, but his angels are not mentioned. However, we see them in the following passages:

Isaiah 24:22:

> **They** [Satan's angels, "the host of heaven on high" of verse 21] **will be gathered together**
> *Like* **prisoners in the dungeon,**
> **And will be confined in prison;** [after the battle of Armageddon]
> **And after many days** [1000 years] **they *will be* punished.**

The punishment is the same as Satan's: eternity in the lake of fire. We see this has been God's plan for Satan and his angels all along by looking at what Jesus will say to the unbelieving Gentiles on His return, as prophesied by Jesus Himself in **Matthew 25:41: "Then He will also say to those on His left, 'Depart from Me, accursed ones, into <u>the eternal fire which has been prepared for the devil and his angels</u>....'"**

F. *After the battle of Armageddon, we are told that all surviving unbelieving mortals (people) are "taken" (killed), while we are not specifically told what happens to the unbelieving mortals who survive the battle of Gog and Magog.*

Many mortals who are part of the invading armies are killed in both battles. After the battle of Armageddon, the remaining unbelievers on earth are killed at the subsequent judgments, as we saw in Chapter 11, "Christ Returns to Rule."

We are not told when unbelievers remaining after this final battle of Gog and Magog are killed, but when the universe is destroyed (how soon after that battle we do not know) that seems to be the only possible scenario, as discussed in the next chapter.

2. Are the battles described in Ezekiel (chapters 38 and 39) and Revelation 20:7-10 the same battle?

Although Bible scholars do not confuse the battle of Armageddon with the battle of Gog and Magog, they often reach the conclusion that the battle of Gog and

Magog described in Ezekiel 38 and 39 is not the same battle as this final battle described in Revelation 20:7-10. However, a close examination of Ezekiel 38 and 39 strongly indicates that the passage in Ezekiel describes the same battle referred to in Revelation 20:7-10. Consider the following:

A. *The names of the invaders of Israel are the same, Gog and Magog.*

Ezekiel 38:2 and 3 reveal that Gog is from the land of Magog, and the same words, **Gog and Magog**, are used to describe the invaders in Revelation 20:8, quoted above. A meaningless coincidence? Not a characteristic of the Word of God.

B. *The description of the land of Israel given before the battle of Gog and Magog in Ezekiel 38 can only be describing the transformed Israel of the millennial kingdom.*

Ezekiel 38:8: [the word of the LORD telling Ezekiel what to prophesy against Gog, which continues throughout Ezekiel 38 and 39] **"After many days you** [Gog] **will be summoned** [by the LORD, v.4]**; in the latter years you will come into the land that is restored from the sword, *whose inhabitants* have been gathered from many nations to the mountains of Israel which had been a continual waste; but its people were brought out from the nations, and they are living securely, all of them."**

Ezekiel 38:11-13: "and you [Gog] **will say, 'I will go up against the land of unwalled** [*i.e.,* unprotected] **villages. I will go against those who are at rest, that live securely, all of them living without walls and having no bars or gates, to capture spoil and to seize plunder, to turn your hand against the waste places which are *now* inhabited, and against the people who are gathered from the nations, who have acquired cattle and goods, who live at the center of the world.' Sheba and Dedan and the merchants of Tarshish with all its villages will say to you, 'Have you come to capture spoil? Have you assembled your company to seize plunder, to carry away silver and gold, to take away cattle and goods, to capture great spoil?'"**

These passages contain a great deal of evidence that the Israel being invaded by Gog in Ezekiel 38 and 39 is the regathered and restored Israel of the millennial kingdom. Since the world and Israel are at peace during Christ's one thousand year reign, this battle can only take place at the end of that time, when Satan is released in Revelation 20:7-10, quoted at the start of the chapter.

Let's take a closer look at the evidence these passages reveal:

(1) The land (Israel) is **restored from the sword.** (v.8)

Not only is Israel at peace for one thousand years, but we saw that the land itself is restored during the millennial kingdom. While the nation of Israel has been working at restoring the land of Israel since 1948, that restoration is nothing compared to the one described for Israel in the millennial kingdom, as we saw in the previous chapter.

> (2) Israel's **inhabitants have been gathered from many nations to the mountains of Israel...its people were brought out from the nations**.... (v.8)

Gog will purpose to go **against the people who are gathered from the nations.** (v.12) This regathering of the nation of Israel takes place at the Christ's return, prior to the start of the millennial kingdom, as we saw in the previous chapter entitled "Christ Returns to Rule." Many of the Jewish people have returned to Israel since 1948, but the present return to the land of Israel falls far short of the promised event which will take place when Christ returns to rule, at which time <u>all</u> believing Jewish people are regathered by God and placed in the land. Furthermore, what is taking place in Israel today is a <u>return</u>, not the promised <u>regathering</u> by God described in so many Biblical prophecies (See Chapter 11, "Christ Returns to Rule".)

> (3) The inhabitants of the land of Israel **are living securely, all of them. (Ezekiel 38:8, 11)**

Can this refer to a time either prior to the start of the Tribulation, or during the first half of the Tribulation, when the people of Israel <u>think</u> they are living securely because of their treaty with the Antichrist? Not really. The passages in Ezekiel 38 don't say that. They say the people of Israel <u>are</u> living securely, <u>all of them</u>. No guessing, wishing or thinking about it. An Israel living in security has not happened since the reign of Solomon, and will not happen again, according to Bible prophecy, until the millennial kingdom.

> (4) The people of Israel **live at the center of the world.** (v.12).

Israel will not be **the center of the world** until Christ rules from the millennial temple in Jerusalem during the millennial kingdom. As we saw in the preceding chapter, Israel becomes the governmental, worship and economic center of the world during the millennial kingdom.

> (5) Gog is thought to be coming **to seize plunder, to carry away silver and gold, to take away cattle and goods, to capture great spoil.** (v.13).

Israel's great wealth during the millennial kingdom is described in the preceding chapter. The invasions of Israel since 1948 have all been motivated by a hatred of the Jewish people. Plunder was never an issue, and is not foremost in minds of Israel's enemies to this day. After **the wealth of the nations** is gathered to Israel during its 1000 years as the world's economic center, plunder will become a much more viable motive for invasion.

<u>Conclusion:</u> The description of the Israel invaded by Gog in Ezekiel 38 can only refer to the Israel existing at the <u>end</u> of the millennial kingdom, making its

timing the same as that of the battle described in Revelation 20:7-10.

Bible scholars raise this objection to the conclusion: What about the fact that Ezekiel's description of the millennial kingdom continues in Ezekiel 39-47 <u>after</u> the description of this battle? However, a close examination of the last half of chapter 39 shows it to be a restatement of the conditions existing in Israel prior to the start of the invasion, as described in the first half of Ezekiel 38. The succeeding chapters 40-48 describe primarily the millennial temple, with its specific dimensions and worship ceremonies, followed by a division of the land among the twelve tribes, with areas reserved for the holy precincts.

These chapters do <u>not</u> present themselves as being in any chronological order. If they were in chronological order, for example, why doesn't the description of the millennial temple (which presumably is constructed or created at the <u>start</u> of the millennium) precede the description of Israel's blessings <u>during</u> the 1000 years? And why is the division of the land (which must take place at the <u>start</u> of the 1000 years) not described until Ezekiel 48? Furthermore, if chronological order is being sought, consider that much of Ezekiel chapters 34-37, <u>preceding</u> description of the battle, are filled with prophecies concerning the regathering of Israel and the blessings of Israel in the millennial kingdom.

   C. *The descriptions of the invading armies are similar.*

Ezekiel 38:9: [Ezekiel prophesying **"Thus says the Lord GOD,"** v. 3] **"You** [Gog] **will go up, you will come like a storm; you will be like a cloud covering the land** [Israel]**, you and all your troops, and many peoples with you."**

We see a similar great army in **Revelation 20:8b-9a: [T]he number of them is like the sand of the seashore. And they came up on the broad plain of the earth and surrounded the camp of the saints and the beloved city....**

   D. *God destroys the armies invading Israel in a similar manner.*

In **Revelation 20:9**, we read that **fire came down from heaven and destroyed them.** The destruction on the invading army is described in **Ezekiel 38:22:** [Ezekiel prophesying "Thus says the Lord GOD," v. 3] **"With pestilence and with blood I shall enter into judgment with him** [Gog]**; and I shall rain on him and his troops, and on the many peoples who are with him, a torrential rain, with hailstone, <u>fire and brimstone</u>."** The passage in Ezekiel gives more detail, with the description of the entire event covering chapters 38 and 39 of Ezekiel. Revelation 20:7-10 appears to be the abbreviated account, without the details.

   E. *There is no other place where the battle described in Ezekiel 38 and 39 fit in the Revelation prophecy of end times, except in the description given in Revelation 20:7-10.*

Important events prophesied about Israel are seldom given in only one place. The account given in Revelation 20:7-10 seems to be an abridged version of the description given in Ezekiel 38 and 39. Revelation 20:7-10 gives us the timing of the battle.

Furthermore, the outline and time frame of all significant events occurring during **the day of the LORD** is given in the book of Revelation, and Revelation 20:7-10 is the only place where a battle similar to the battle of Gog and Magog is mentioned, yet we know Ezekiel's battle of Gog and Magog takes place **in the latter years** (**Ezekiel 38:8**) and **in the last days** (**Ezekiel 38:16**), both referencing an end times event.

Conclusion: All of these clues point to the conclusion that Ezekiel 38 and 39 and Revelation 20:7-10 are describing the same battle.

F. *Difficulties with the conclusion.*

There are three apparent differences in the two descriptions that present some difficulty:

(1) Gog's armies in Ezekiel come out of the north, while the army in **Revelation 20:8** comes from nations **in the four corners of the earth.**

In Ezekiel's description of the battle, all the nations mentioned by name that attack Israel come from the north, while the attacking army in **Revelation 20:8** comes from **the four corners of the earth.** However, the fact that **Ezekiel 38:9 and 15** both say to Gog that he will have **many peoples with you** [Gog], indicates that the army could include countries not listed as part of the invading army.

(2) There is a seven-year time period after the battle in Ezekiel 39, but no such time period is mentioned in Revelation 20:7-10.

After the battle described by Ezekiel, the people of Israel burn the weapons of the destroyed army for seven years (Ezekiel 39:9). We don't see a space of seven years after this battle in Revelation 20, which transitions from the destruction of the invading army in Revelation 20:9 straight to the destruction of the universe in **Revelation 20:11: Then I saw a great white throne and Him who sat upon it, <u>from whose presence earth and heaven fled away, and no place was found for them.</u>**

The seven-year time period after the battle is not mentioned in Revelation or anywhere else in Scripture. However, nowhere does Scripture say that the earth is destroyed <u>immediately</u> after this final battle. Furthermore, there appears no other logical place where this battle could occur **in the latter years** and **in the last days** (**Ezekiel 38:8, 16**).

(3) In Ezekiel, God brings out Gog and his army, while in Revelation, Satan gathers the army to invade Israel.

In **Ezekiel 38:4**, the LORD says to Gog, **"I will bring you out, and all your army...."** In Revelation 20:8, Satan gathers the nations for the war. This could indicate two different battles or, according to this conclusion, it could indicate that once again God is using Satan to accomplish His divine purpose, as He used the beast (antichrist) and his ten kings in **Revelation 17:17:** [one of the seven angels who had the seven bowl speaking to John in his vision, v.1] **"For God has put it in their hearts to execute His purpose...."**

Conclusion: The timing and context of many of the Old Testament prophecies was not made clear until the book of Revelation was written. Contrary to what we see in many commentaries, John's prophecy in Revelation 20:7-9 gives us the timing for the battle of Gog and Magog described in Ezekiel 38-39, specifically mentioning Gog and Magog in verse 8. The entire army of rebellious mortals are killed, and Satan and his fallen angels are doomed to eternity in the lake of fire.

FOR REVIEW: (Cite verses for your answers.)

1. When does this final battle between God and Satan happen? _____

2. Where does this final battle happen? _____

3. What happens to Satan and his angels after this battle? _____

4. What happens to all the mortals who fight in this battle? _____

5. Do you think the battle described in Revelation 20 and the one described in Ezekiel 38 and 39 are the same battle? Why or why not?
_____
_____

6. Name the ways in which this final battle differs from the battle of Armageddon.
_____

7. What does this final battle say to you about mankind's relationship with God?
_____

8. Why is it that after 1000 years of perfect rule on a restored earth, the battle of Gog and Magog still takes place?
_____

CHAPTER FIFTEEN
THE GREAT WHITE THRONE

MAIN IDEA: Jesus sits on a great white throne, while the entire universe is burned up, and all unbelievers from every age are resurrected and appear before Him for judgment. All are thrown into the lake of fire because their names do not appear in the book of life. Unbelievers do not spend eternity in Hell, or Hades, but in the lake of fire.

We come now to the saddest chapter in the book, the one that describes the eternal fate of all unbelievers. Who among us does not have unbelieving friends for whom we pray and to whom we witness at every opportunity? The thought of them spending eternity in a lake of fire is both motivating and saddening. In **2 Peter 2:9**, we read that God keeps **the unrighteous under punishment** [in torment in Hades; see Luke 16:19-25] **for the day of judgment.** That day of judgment is described in **Revelation 20:11-15:**

Then I saw a great white throne and Him who sat upon it, from whose presence earth and heaven fled away, and no place was found for them. And I saw the dead, the great and the small, standing before the throne, and books were opened; and another book was opened; which is *the book* of life; and the dead were judged from the things which were written in the books, according to their deeds. And the sea gave up the dead which were in it, and death and Hades gave up the dead which were in them; and they were judged, every one *of them* according to their deeds. Then death and Hades were thrown into the lake of fire. This is the second [*i.e.,* spiritual] **death, the lake of fire. And if anyone's name was not found written in the book of life, he was thrown into the lake of fire.**

These five verses contain a great deal of information which must be categorized and examined individually. Here we see the destruction of the present universe, the Son of God sitting in judgment of the unbelieving dead, who are resurrected in immortal bodies, judged and found wanting, and condemned to **the lake of fire** for all eternity, referred to as **the second death**. The only bright spot in this picture occurs in verse 14, where **death and Hades were thrown into the lake of fire.**

1. *The destruction of the present universe.*

Verse 11 above says, **from whose presence earth and heaven fled away.** They are gone forever. This should not come as a surprise to those who are even vaguely acquainted with the physics behind the "Big Bang" theory of the origin of the universe. According to this author's understanding of Einstein's calculations, time, space and matter can only co-exist in this present creation.

According to the theory, no two can exist independently of the third. God created all three simultaneously when He created the universe, and if one is removed, the other two must be also. Keep in mind that God has always existed outside of time, in eternity past before the creation of the universe, in what some Bible scholars call "the eternal present," exists outside of time now, and will always exist outside of time in eternity future. He is outside the universe in the sense that He is not part of it. (Thus those who seek evidence of God Himself in the universe will always be disappointed.)

We learn that the destruction comes by fire in **2 Peter 3:7, 10:**

But by His [Christ's] **word the present heavens and earth are being reserved for fire, kept for the day of judgment and the destruction of ungodly men** [i.e., the great white throne judgment]**.... But the day of the Lord will come like a thief, in which the heavens will pass away with a roar and the elements will be destroyed with intense heat, and the earth and its works will be burned up.**

Jesus Himself said in His Olivet Discourse that **"Heaven and earth will pass away, but My words will not pass away." Matthew 24:35, Mark 13:31, Luke 21:33.**

The fact that the present universe is totally destroyed is confirmed in **Revelation 21:1: ...for the first heaven and the first earth passed away....**

If the entire universe is burned up, what happens to the people living on the earth at that time? Short answer: The Bible does not tell us. However, from what we know of the character and promises of God, it seems very unlikely that believers will be burned up in that final fire, but instead will somehow be removed beforehand.

2. *Jesus, the Son of God, is the one sitting in judgment on the great white throne.*

John 5:25-29: [Jesus speaking] **"Truly, truly, I say to you, an hour is coming and now is, when the dead will hear the voice of the Son of God, and those who hear will live. For just as the Father has life in Himself, even so He gave to the Son also to have life in Himself; and He** [the Father] **gave Him** [the Son] **authority to execute judgment, because He is the Son of Man. Do not marvel at this; for an hour is coming, in which all who are in the tombs will hear His** [the Son's] **voice, and will come forth; those who did the good** *deeds* [i.e., believers] **to a resurrection of** [eternal] **life, <u>those who committed the evil *deeds*** [*i.e.,* unbelievers] **to a resurrection of judgment.</u>"**

John 5: 22: [Jesus speaking] **"For not even the Father judges anyone, but He has given all judgment to the Son...."**

Acts 10:42: [the apostle Peter speaking] **"[T]his is the One** [Jesus] **who has been appointed by God as Judge of the** [spiritually] **living and the**

[spiritually] **dead."**

3. *The unbelieving dead are resurrected.*

After talking about the resurrection of believers at Christ's return to rule, John tells us in **Revelation 20:5a: The rest of the dead** [*i.e.*, all unbelievers] **did not come to life until the thousand years** [the millennial kingdom] **was completed.**

As discussed above, all unbelievers will be dead at the start of this judgment when the present universe is destroyed. Statements in Revelation 20:11-15 (quoted at the beginning of the chapter) indicate that the dead unbelievers will be resurrected for this judgment. In verse 12 we see them all <u>**standing** before the **throne.**</u> The resurrection is described in detail in **Revelation 20:13: "And the sea** [apparently the Gentile nations, see Revelation 17:15] **gave up the dead** [<u>bodies</u>] **which were in it, and death and Hades gave up the dead** [<u>souls</u>] **which were in them...."** This reuniting of body and soul is, of course, a resurrection.

The song sung in the land of Judah during the millennial kingdom contains these lines in **Isaiah 26:14:**
   The [spiritually] **dead will not live, the departed spirits will not rise**
      [until after the millennial kingdom]**;**
   Therefore You have wiped out all remembrance of them.

As we saw previously, all mortal unbelievers will be killed at the start of the millennial kingdom, awaiting this day of judgment. There is good news here for believers, though. It seems that believers in the millennial kingdom will have no remembrance of their unbelieving loved ones, and therefore will not mourn their fate. Neither will they be remembered in eternity: **Isaiah 65:17:** [the Lord GOD speaking, v.13]

> **"For behold, I create a new heavens and a new earth,**
> **And <u>the former things shall not be remembered or come to mind</u>...."**

4. *The resurrected bodies of unbelievers will not be destroyed in the lake of fire.*

A resurrection unites a dead body which has been restored to life with its soul. In the case of the believing dead resurrected at the rapture, the dead bodies are transformed into living "glorified" bodies, in some ways apparently similar to Christ's resurrected body. This passage in Revelation 20 does not describe the resurrected bodies of the unbelievers, but we know that they will not be totally destroyed in the lake of fire, since their torment never ends:

Revelation 14:9-11: Then another angel, a third one, followed them, saying with a loud voice, "If anyone worships the beast and his image, and receives a mark on his forehead or on his hand, he also will drink of the wine of the wrath of God, which is mixed in full strength in the cup of His

anger; and he will be <u>tormented with fire and brimstone</u> in the presence of the holy angels and in the presence of the Lamb. And <u>the smoke of their torment goes up forever and ever</u>; they have no rest day and night, those who worship the beast and his image, and whoever receives the mark of his name."

Isaiah 66:24: [the LORD speaking]

**"Then they shall go forth and look
On the corpses of the men
Who have transgressed against Me.
For <u>their worm shall not die</u>
<u>And their fire shall not be quenched;</u>
And they shall be an abhorrence to all mankind."**

These last words of warning in the book of Isaiah, while confirming that the unbeliever's torment will have no end, give us a glimpse of the unbelievers' resurrected bodies. They are called **corpses**, and referred to as **their worm**. Nothing like the "glorified bodies" of believers. These passages also tell us that these bodies will be capable of feeling **torment.** In the picture of the rich man in the place of torment described by Jesus, even before receiving his resurrected body, the rich man says, **"I am in agony in this flame."** Luke 16:24b.

5. *The resurrected unbelievers are judged "according to their deeds," and found wanting.*

In **Revelation 20:12, the books are opened... and the** [spiritually] **dead were judged from the things written in the books, according to their deeds.** The word "deeds" can be interpreted to mean (1) everything a person has done, whether considered "good" or "bad" in the eyes of men, or (2) only things considered "good" in the eyes of men, since Christ died for the "bad" things, the sins, or (3) only things viewed as "good" in the eyes of God, since these are the only deeds valued by God, and Christ already paid the penalty for all sin on the cross. <u>The point of opening the books of their deeds is to show that no one can enter eternity with God (what we call "heaven") on the basis of their deeds.</u>

We are not told which standard Jesus applies at this judgment. John 3:16, 2 Peter 3:9 and many other verses imply that Jesus died to pay for the sins of all mankind. Since all sin is already paid for, sin should not be the issue. If so, either option (2) or (3) appear to be the likely standard for this judgment. If option (3) is the standard, the books containing the deeds of unbelievers will be empty, based on Jesus' words in **John 15:5: "I am the vine, you are the branches; he who abides in Me and I in him, he bears much fruit, for <u>apart from Me you can do nothing</u>."**

We also know from **Isaiah 26:12** that the LORD (YHWH, *i.e.,* Jesus) performs for us **all our works.** Unbelievers are not "in Christ," and Christ does not dwell in them. They are therefore incapable of performing "good" deeds in the eyes of God, since God does not indwell them and will perform no works through them. (This is not to say that God cannot or does not use unbelievers to accomplish His purpose, *e.g.,* the ten kings in Revelation 17:17 and Cyrus in Isaiah 44:28.)

For the same reason, if option (2) is the standard, all of the unbelievers' **deeds**, considered good in the eyes of men, will still be worthless in the Judge's eyes, comparable to the **wood, hay, straw**, the believers' works burned up at the judgment seat of Christ in **1 Corinthians 3:10-15**. Whatever standard Jesus applies, and whatever is written in the books, one fact will become evident to every unbeliever standing before the throne: They can do nothing to merit their own salvation.

All unbelievers will then understand that accepting Jesus' free gift of salvation, which He purchased at so great a cost on the cross, was their only hope, and they did not receive that free gift. Because they did not accept His gift, none of their names appear in the other book which is opened, the book of life. In verse 15, they all are thrown into the lake of fire, joining the antichrist and his false prophet, (Rev. 19:20 Satan (Rev. 20:10) and his angels (Isaiah 24:22, Matt.25:41), and death and Hades (Rev. 20:14). The saddest day in the history of the world will not compare to this moment.

FOR REVIEW: (Cite verses for your answers)

1. Who is sitting on the great white throne? _____

2. Is the great white throne located in the present universe? _____

3. How do we know the present universe is destroyed at the time of the great white throne judgment?
_____

4. How is this present universe destroyed? _____

5. BONUS QUESTION: Why do you think God's plan includes destruction of this universe?
_____

6. Who appears before the great white throne to be judged? _____

7. Are those judged at the great white throne judgment in spirit form, or do they have resurrected bodies?
_____

8. What are the books that are opened? _____

9. What happens to all who are judged? _____

10. What causes them to receive that judgment? _____

11. Name all who are mentioned in Revelation 19 and 20 as being thrown into the lake of fire._____

_____

12. So what does a person have to do to spend eternity with God ("get to heaven")?
_____

_____

CHAPTER SIXTEEN
ETERNITY IN THE NEW JERUSALEM

MAIN IDEA: All believers spend a joyful eternity in their immortal, glorified bodies serving God in the new Jerusalem, which comes down from heaven to a new earth. Believers do not spend eternity in heaven, but in the new Jerusalem on the new earth.

In chapter one, we saw that when believers die, they go directly into the presence of God in the already created new Jerusalem in heaven. Most of what the Bible tells us about this heavenly city is described in Revelation 21 and 22. Turn there in your Bible as you go through this chapter.

We start with this description from **Revelation 21:1-4:**

Then I saw a new heaven and a new earth; for the first heaven and the first earth passed away, and there is no longer *any* sea. And I saw the holy city, new Jerusalem, coming down out of heaven from God, made ready as a bride adorned for her husband. And I heard a loud voice from the throne, saying, "Behold, the tabernacle of God is among men, and He will dwell among them, and they shall be His people, and God himself will be among them, and he will wipe away every tear from their eyes; and there will no longer be *any* death; there will no longer be *any* mourning, or crying, or pain; the first things have passed away."

Isaiah saw a similar vision, recounted in **Isaiah 65:17-19:** [the Lord GOD speaking, v.13]

> "For behold, I create new heavens and a new earth;
> And the former things shall not be remembered or come to mind.
> But be glad and rejoice forever in what I create;
> For behold, I create a Jerusalem *for* rejoicing and her people *for*
>   gladness.
> I will also rejoice in Jerusalem and be glad in My people;
> And there will no longer be heard in her
> The voice of weeping and the sound of crying."

After the destruction of this present universe, we see a new one created (made out of nothing, not made out of reassembled material from the old universe). Then comes the picture of the **new Jerusalem, coming down out of heaven from God**. (**Revelation 21:2**) The implication is that this new Jerusalem comes down to the new earth, but since this is not explicitly stated, many assume that the heavenly city will somehow remain suspended above the new earth for eternity. The description that follows in Revelation 21 and 22 does not support that concept, but instead seems to speak of the new Jerusalem as being situated on the new earth.

Revelation 21:10-22:5 describe a city with a wall having foundation stones and twelve gates guarded by angels, all of which would be pointless in a city floating in the sky for eternity. We read in **Revelation 21:24-26: The nations will walk by its light, and the kings of the earth will bring their glory into it. In the daytime (for there will be no night there) its gates will never be closed; and they will bring the glory and the honor of the nations into it;....** This sounds like a city actually located on the new earth.

Israel will exist in the eternal state. Many passages in the Old Testament make it clear that God's promises to Israel are eternal, not just for the 1000 year millennial kingdom. For example, **Ezekiel 37:25-26:** [the word of the LORD, v.15] **"They** ["the sons of Israel," v.21] **shall live on the land that I gave to Jacob My servant, in which your fathers lived; and they will live on it, they, and their sons and their sons' sons, forever; and David My servant shall be their prince forever. I will make a covenant of peace with them; it will be an everlasting covenant with them. And I will place them and multiply them, and will set My sanctuary in their midst forever."**

While this passage deals primarily with the millennial kingdom, it clearly indicates that the nation of Israel will exist in eternity. The same thought is in these verses:

Isaiah 66:22: [the LORD speaking, v.21]
  "For just as the new heavens and the new earth
  Which I make will endure before Me," declares the LORD,
  "So your offspring and your name [Israel] **will endure."**

Isaiah 60:19-21a: [the LORD speaking, 59:21]
  "No longer will you have the sun for light by day,
  Nor for brightness will the moon give you light;
  But you will have the LORD for an everlasting light,
  And your God for your glory.
  Your sun will set no more;
  Neither will your moon wane;
  For you will have the LORD for an everlasting light,
  And the days of your mourning will be finished.
  Then all your [Israel's] **people *will be* righteous;**
  They will possess the land forever."

If Israel is to exist in eternity, its capital will be the new Jerusalem. The eternal nation of Israel must exist on the new earth, and it seems probable that its capital will also.

Israel will apparently not be the only nation in the eternal state on the new earth, as we saw in Revelation 21:24, quoted above. We see references to other nations on the new earth in Revelation 22:2, Ezekiel 37:28, and possibly Isaiah 60:22, but we are not given any details.

The description of the new Jerusalem is so wonderful it is beyond our comprehension. The details given are limited to those we can understand, and even then some of the things described are inexplicable. It is called **the city of the living God, the heavenly Jerusalem. Hebrews 12:22.**

Here are some of the things we are told about the new Jerusalem:

1. The new Jerusalem already exists in heaven. (Hebrews 11:10,16; 12:22)

2. The new Jerusalem is in the shape of a cube, 1380 (translated 1500 in some translations) miles in length, width and height. (Revelation 21:16) A city this tall would not be physically possible on the present earth; either the new earth will be much bigger or God will change His laws of physics.

3. The city wall is 72 feet thick and made of precious stones: 12 foundation stones of different precious stones bearing the names of the 12 apostles (each apparently approximately 460 miles long and 72 feet wide, of unrevealed height); topped by a wall of **crystal clear jasper**, thought to be diamond. (**Revelation 21:11, 18**)

4. The city has 12 gates, each made from a single pearl, three gates on each side of the city, each gate bearing the name of a tribe of Israel. An angel will be standing at each gate. (Revelation 21:12, 21)

5. The city has a street of **pure gold, like transparent glass. (Revelation 21:21**) Exactly how does that work? We will know when we get there.

6. The city will be illuminated by the glory of God [the Father] and the Lamb, whose throne will be in it. (Revelation 21:3,23; 22:1,3,5)

7. A **river of the water of life** will come from the throne of God and the Lamb and flow **in the middle of its street. (Revelation 22:1,2a**), reminiscent of the river flowing out of Eden in Genesis 2:10.

8. **On either side of the river was the tree of life, ... Revelation 22:2.** The need for the fruit of the tree of life and exactly how its leaves heal the nations is not revealed, but it appears to be the same tree of life that was in the garden of Eden mentioned in Genesis 2:9,22,24.

9. There God's bond-servants **will see His face, and His name *will be* on their foreheads. Revelation 22:4.**

10. The city will be free of sin and unbelievers. (Revelation 21:27; 22:14,15). We will have no memory of them to cloud our joy. Speaking of unbelievers, Isaiah prophesied in **Isaiah 26:14:**
   The dead will not live, the departed spirits will not rise;

**Therefore You have punished and destroyed them.
And You have wiped out all remembrance of them.**

11. The curse resulting from sin will be gone. (Revelation 21:4; 22:3)

In the quotation at the first of the chapter from **Revelation 21:1-4**, John sees the new Jerusalem **coming down out of heaven from God.** At this time, all believers from every age will be dwelling in the new Jerusalem, and will no doubt be in it as it descends to the new earth.

As revealed in the list above, the pearly gates of heaven are actually the twelve open gates of the new Jerusalem, with each gate made of a single pearl, and the "streets of gold" in heaven turn out to be a single street in the new Jerusalem of, yes, pure gold (Revelation 21:21). We don't find "Saint Peter" at any of the pearly gates, however; instead we find an angel at each gate (Revelation 21:12). Peter's name is not even on any of the gates, which bear instead the names of the twelve tribes (sons) of Israel. His name is, however, on one of the twelve foundation stones of the city wall, along with the names of the other eleven **apostles of the Lamb.** (**Revelation 21:14**). There is no point speculating about whether the twelfth apostle will be Matthais or Paul. We will know when we read the names.

There will be no need of a sun or moon; light for the city and the entire new earth will come from the light of God's glory, as we saw in Isaiah 60:19-21a, quoted above, also mentioned in Revelation 21:23-25, 22:5. **The throne of God and the Lamb will be in it** [the new Jerusalem].... **Revelation 22:3.** It is hard to imagine the beauty and glory of this giant jewel shining the light of God's glory into the new universe.

Christians wonder: Will we be united with our loved ones? Will we even recognize anyone in the new Jerusalem? A definitive answer is not given, but the inference drawn from several verses indicate that the answer to both questions is yes. Consider **Isaiah 26:14**, quoted above. The very fact that we will have **no remembrance** of unbelievers indicates we will remember the believers we knew on this earth. How could we live in gladness and joy (Revelation 21:1-4 and Isaiah 65:17-19, quoted above), remembering our loved ones and not being reunited?

The story Jesus tells of Lazarus and the rich man in Luke 16:19-31 tells us that we will recognize people we knew on earth and we will be able to communicate. **Luke 16:23:** [Jesus speaking] **"In Hades, he [the rich man] lifted up his eyes, being in torment, and saw Abraham far away and Lazarus in his bosom."** If even the unbelieving rich man can recognize Lazarus **far away**, whom he knew on earth, and Abraham, whom he probably never met, it seems very likely that we will recognize and be united with our loved ones. Notice that Abraham, in Paradise (See Luke 23:41) prior to the resurrection, can speak and hear, *i.e.,* communicate. Remember, these are the words of Jesus Himself. He would know what the spirit realm is like.

But the ability to recognize and communicate with others in eternity appears to go beyond recognizing those believers we knew in this life. Notice that even the unbelieving rich man can recognize Abraham, although there is no indication he lived when Abraham lived, and his lifestyle indicates that he lived much later. At the transfiguration (Matthew 17:1-8), Peter, James and John instantly recognized Moses and Elijah in their glorified state, although both had departed this world hundreds of years before, and the Jews, for fear of violating the prohibition against graven images, had no pictures or statues of what they looked like.

The inference is that we will be able to recognize at least those saints of whom we have heard, and perhaps we will be able to recognize <u>everyone</u> in the new Jerusalem. Either way, it seems we will recognize our loved ones who are there, and have **no remembrance** of those who are not.

The new earth and the new Jerusalem will be inhabited by all the unfallen angels and all the saints from every age. We will not be sitting around on clouds playing harps, however. We (believers from every age) are the bond-servants of Christ. We see this in Paul's instruction to Timothy on shepherding the church at Ephesus given in **2 Timothy 2:24: The Lord's <u>bond-servant</u> must not be quarrelsome, be kind to all, able to teach, patient when wronged,....** (See also Col. 1:7; 4:7, Acts 16:17).

So what will we, His bondservants, be doing in eternity? **Revelation 22:3b-4,5b: [A]nd His bond-servants will <u>serve</u> Him; <u>they will see His face</u>, and His name** *will be* **on their foreheads....[A]nd they will reign forever and ever.** We will be joyfully serving and reigning with our Lord and Savior.

Ever since the fall described in Genesis 3, mortal mankind has not, with a few exceptions, seen the face of God in His glorified state. Moses asked to see His glory in Exodus 33:18, and was permitted a glimpse in Exodus 34:6, but was not permitted to see His face, **"for no man can see Me and live!" Exodus 33:20b**. Jacob wrestled with God, and then marveled **"I have seen God face to face, yet my life has been preserved." Genesis 32:30.** However, it is not at all clear that Jacob actually saw Christ in His glorified state, since he apparently wrestled with Him appearing as a man (Genesis 32:24). Isaiah saw the preincarnate Christ (see John 12:41) in His glory in Isaiah 6:1-5, and feared for his life, and Ezekiel saw in a vision **the appearance of the likeness of the glory of the Lord (Ezekiel 1:28b)**, and fell on his face. The apostle John saw himself **"in the Spirit: and behold, a throne was standing in heaven, and One sitting on the throne. Revelation 4:2.** And, of course, Peter, James and John apparently saw the glorified Jesus at the transfiguration.

In eternity in the new Jerusalem, we, as immortals, <u>will see His face</u>, fulfilling the wonderful priestly blessing of **Numbers 6:24-26:**

The Lord bless you, and keep you;

**The LORD make His face shine on you,
And be gracious to you;
The LORD lift us His countenance on you,
And give you peace.**

Think about it. We will spend eternity with all believers from every age and all God's angels in the presence of our God and Savior. He will have a use for us; we will have the opportunity to serve Him. We will live in God's light and see His face, in a place without death and with no more **"mourning, or crying, or pain;"** (**Revelation 21:4**), a place of **rejoicing** and **gladness** for all eternity (**Isaiah 65:17-19**, quoted above). But most of all, we will live in the light, glory and love of our Creator and Redeemer, in His very presence. And we **will see His face.** Nothing else will matter….

FOR REVIEW: (Cite verses for your answers.)

1. Where do believers spend eternity? _____

2. What is our ultimate purpose in eternity? _____
_____

3. What will you remember about your unbelieving friends and relatives in eternity?
_____

4. When was/is the new Jerusalem apparently created? _____
_____

5. When was/is the new heaven and new earth apparently created? _____
_____

6. What will your emotions be in eternity? _____

7. Will there be any death on the new earth? _____

8. List some of the things we are told about the new Jerusalem. _____
_____
_____

9. What are you looking forward to most in eternity? _____
_____

ACKNOWLEDGEMENTS

My heartfelt thanks to (now retired) Pastors Bruce Miles and Dwight George of Rocky Mountain Bible Church in Frisco, Colorado, whose excellent Bible scholarship and teaching over the last 16 years provided me the Biblical foundation for this book. That being said, neither of them edited this book, and not all conclusions set forth in the book should be attributed to them.

My understanding of (1) the meaning of "earth dwellers" and "heaven dwellers", (2) "the beginning of birth pangs" in Matthew 24:5-9a and Revelation 6, and (3) the appearance of the raptured church in Revelation 7, I owe totally to my friend and former pastor, Dr. A. Boyd Luter (Ph. D, Dallas Theological Seminary) and his excellent paper, "Earth Dwellers and Heaven Dwellers". It literally "opened my eyes" to understanding the chronological order of events in the book of Revelation.

I also want to thank my friends who comprised my informal "editorial board" and greatly improved this second edition of *THE DAY OF THE LORD*: Jim and Evelyn Rogers, Bob and Sandy Pawalko, Dennis Burt, and especially my friend of over half a century who served as my layman editor, Rod Miller.

A special thanks to my friend Nancy Schaffer, who provided invaluable technical support to solve several computer glitches I encountered while writing this book.

My wife, Naomi Nolan, spent countless hours proofreading and editing the first edition of *The Day of the Lord*, and has been an unfailing supporter, encourager and proofreader of the revisions included in this second edition. She has endured without complaint the time I have spent on writing both the first and second editions, for which I will always be grateful.

Made in the USA
San Bernardino, CA
02 April 2016